𝔗𝔥𝔢 𝔇𝔞𝔦𝔩𝔶 𝔗𝔢𝔩𝔢𝔤𝔯𝔞𝔭𝔥
Winning Bridge
at Home

Tony Forrester

D0048015

B. T. Batsford Ltd, *London*

First published 1996

© Tony Forrester 1996

ISBN 0 7134 7780 6

A CIP catalogue record for this book is available from the British Library.

Typeset by Apsbridge Services Ltd, Nottingham.
Printed by Redwood Books, Trowbridge, Wiltshire
for the publishers,
B. T. Batsford Ltd, 4 Fitzhardinge Street,
London W1H 0AH

A BATSFORD BRIDGE BOOK
Series Editor: Tony Sowter

CONTENTS

INTRODUCTION

This Series of Books is Dedicated to
My wife Diana
Who has been my Inspiration

This book, despite being the last in a series of three, is nevertheless one which will stand on its own. It is designed to take the 'average' home bridge player into the category of a 'winning' player.

However, as with my earlier two books, *Play Bridge at Home* and *Improve Your Bridge at Home* I intend to develop your expertise without recourse to unnecessary complexities.

I will outline the basic 'Acol' or 'Natural' system and show how we can bid slams accurately. I will arm you with the ammunition to fight competitive sequences and win the war. You will see some of the more common advanced techniques in card play.

Finally, you can look forward to defending with new-found confidence after reading the section on 'Advanced Signalling'. All in all, a lot to get through, but as always I will err on the side of caution when it comes to the speed with which I will tackle new concepts. In bridge, the old adage holds good – 'A little learning is a dangerous thing'. A half-understood idea is more likely to cost points than benefit you in the long term.

I should know, I see it all the time at Tournament level, when International players get absurd results because one of them has forgotten a rarely used part of his system. I don't want you getting into bad habits!

1
LOW-LEVEL COMPETITION

You have just started a new rubber and picked up your cards with eager anticipation. Your left hand opponent opens 1NT, partner passes and your right hand opponent raises to 3NT. Are you excited, interested, on the edge of your seat? Hardly!

The only way I could ever imagine abandoning my true love of playing bridge is if you told me that in future every sequence would be similarly unenterprising. Fortunately that will never happen.

The life blood of bidding is the competitive auction where both sides are jockeying for position. No longer are we simply faced with an objective assessment of our general strength and suitability as in sequences where we are 'left alone'. Now we have another fascinating dimension. What are our opponents trying to do and how can we get the better of them? Risk and reward are at their height when we get involved in the thrust and parry of a competitive sequence: a mistake can cost a fortune, but a successful manoeuvre spells profit. We must arm ourselves for the struggle, so it is time to load our pistols and await the dawn.

• • • • •

To make an auction 'competitive' requires someone at the table to make an overcall, i.e. to suggest that the side who opened the bidding has no God-given right to declare the final contract. It seems sensible then for us to start by examining the requirements for an overcall and what we are attempting to achieve by 'poking our noses' into the bidding.

I believe we can summarise the possible reasons for entering the auction as follows:

1. We have a realistic expectation that our side has the overall balance of strength and can therefore make a contract somewhere. Our overcall must, as with an opening bid, be a first step in determining where our best resting place may be.

2. We may be able to push the opponents around and force them higher than they wish to go. This will give us a better chance of defeating their contract.

3. We provide our partner with information about our hand which is likely to help in the key choice of an opening lead and with later decisions. In effect, we have guided the defence before it begins.

4. We may cause disruption to our opponents bidding by 'taking up bidding space'. To see the concept more clearly, imagine that an auction is like a conversation with a fairly wide-ranging vocabulary to express yourself. When an opponent overcalls, they remove some of the words from our vocabulary and, the higher they bid, the more words disappear. It becomes increasingly difficult for a player to express himself efficiently.

Here are some examples which illustrate the above principles.

Realistic Expectation of Making a Contract

South has opened the bidding with 1◊, what action do you take on the following hands:

(a)	♠ AK1097	(b)	♠ A6	(c)	♠ KQ107
	♡ KJ73		♡ KJ5		♡ AJ93
	◊ 72		◊ K4		◊ 7
	♣ Q6		♣ AQJ1073		♣ KQ84

All three hands fall into the category of having 'sufficient strength to make a contract'. If we assume that the opener bidding has around 13 points or so, then each of our examples is at least as strong as he is. Therefore, we have a reasonable expectation of holding greater combined high card strength than the opponents. We should be trying for a contract in our direction.

On hand (a) we overcall 1♠ much in line with the action we would take if opening the bidding. Hand (b) could be overcalled 2♣, but a jump overcall of 3♣ expresses the strength better. It is hand (c) where we have a problem. Which one of our four card suits should we bid?

The answer is 'none of them'. It is rarely wise to overcall on a four-card suit and my personal minimum length of suit is as follows:

OVERCALL	NON VULNERABLE	VULNERABLE
1-LEVEL	FIVE	FIVE
2-LEVEL	FIVE*	SIX
3-LEVEL	SIX	SIX*

*You need either a very good suit or a very good hand (15 or more points) or ideally both.

On that basis, our nice three-suited hand cannot bid at all, but that would go against everything I have been saying up to now.

The answer is to 'double'. We will see later how we use double to penalise the opponents, and that is indeed its normal use. However, it does have something of a 'Jekyll and Hyde' existence, as it can equally be used as a 'takeout' bid.

A *takeout double* says 'Bid your best suit partner, I have support for you'. It arises only in situations where the doubler's partner has not made a positive call. So, for example, South is making a takeout double in this sequence:

West	North	East	South
Pass	Pass	1◇	Double

However, in the example below, South is making a penalty double:

West	North	East	South
Pass	1♣	1◇	Double

The reason being that North has opened, thus changing the whole complexion of the bidding. Now *East/West are competing* the hand, whereas in the previous example North/South were.

Here are three typical examples of a takeout double of a 1◇ opening:

(a) ♠ AQ108
    ♡ AQ108
    ◇ 64
    ♣ J107

(b) ♠ KQ107
    ♡ Q98
    ◇ 5
    ♣ AQ1086

(c) ♠ A74
    ♡ QJ109
    ◇ 63
    ♣ AKQ7

In each case you should double to ask for partner's best suit, rather than guess a suit of your own. In effect, by making a takeout double you bid three suits at once! Here are some examples where a takeout double is *not* advisable:

♠ AQ1086	♠ AQ84	♠ 75
♡ J93	♡ J86	♡ AQ984
◇ 64	◇ Q107	◇ J
♣ AJ7	♣ K94	♣ AQ984
Bid 1♠	Pass	Bid 1♡

None of the above have the key ingredient for doubling, *support for the other three suits.*

How do we respond to a takeout double? You are expected to bid no matter how weak you are, because otherwise you will have to try and beat the opponents in a doubled contract when partner has announced that he does *not* have that suit.

When responding, imagine that you facing a minimum opening in your best suit, and go to the highest level of contract which you feel you can make. Here are a few examples:

West	North	East	South
–	–	1◇	Double
Pass	?		

What would you bid as North with:

(a) ♠ 653		**(b)** ♠ 10842		**(c)** ♠ J98	
♡ 9742		♡ 65		♡ 107	
◇ J1098		◇ Q7		◇ Q9	
♣ 65		♣ 108642		♣ AQ10864	

(d) ♠ KJ1094		**(e)** ♠ Q10864		**(f)** ♠ AJ97	
♡ 93		♡ AQ9		♡ AJ97	
◇ A842		◇ K108		◇ 64	
♣ 93		♣ J7		♣ Q108	

My suggestions are as follows:

(a) 1♡. You have been asked for your best suit, and you must oblige. A simple bid does not promise strength as it would if partner had opened 1◊, because in that situation you had the option of passing. Here you do not.

(b) 1♠ or 2♣. There is a choice between 2♣ which is a level higher, but you do have an extra trump, and 1♠. I prefer 1♠ because it keeps the bidding lower and with 2 points that can't be a bad thing!

(c) 3♣. What you would bid if partner opened 1♣.

(d) 2♠ or 3♠. Again, your response to an imagined opening of 1♠ by partner. Whether you prefer a jump to two or three spades is largely a matter of style. 2♠ for the slight under-bidders or 3♠ for the overbidder. If you didn't precisely know how to categorise your approach as an over or under bidder, you do now.

(e) 4♠. You would raise a 1♠ opening bid to game, do so here.

(f) 2◊. A 'cuebid' of the enemy suit. This bid says two things: (1) I have at least the values to go to three level and (2) I have both majors. It is useful as a way to avoid a guess as to which major to play in. Partner should bid his longer major in response to 2◊, or 2♡ if they are equal. Thus you guarantee to find at least a 4-4 fit.

Finally three examples of the type of hand where you should pass your partner's takeout double:

West	North	East	South
–	Pass	1◊	Dble
Pass	?		

As North, you should pass on any of the following:

(a)	♠ 73	(b)	♠ 7	(c)	♠ Q7
	♡ 732		♡ Q98		♡ K53
	◊ KQ10975		◊ AKJ107		◊ QJ10962
	♣ 72		♣ 7653		♣ Q7

As you can see, the diamond suit dominates the hand, then (and only then) can you pass.

Takeout doubles occur in other sequences. Here are some of them:

(a)	West	North	East	South
	–	1◇	Pass	Pass
	Dble			

(b)	West	North	East	South
	–	–	Pass	3◇
	Dble			

(c)	West	North	East	South
	–	1◇	Pass	1♡
	Dble			

(d)	West	North	East	South
	–	1◇	Pass	2◇
	Dble			

All West's doubles are takeout and typically show support for the unbid suits and enough strength to enter the bidding at the appropriate level. A 'classical' example of each double would be:

(a)
♠ AQ107
♡ Q1086
◇ 5
♣ K942

This 'protective' double can afford to be a little lighter because South has passed partner's opening.

(b)
♠ KQ107
♡ KQ107
◇ 5
♣ A952

You need a decent hand to bid at the three level, particularly when you do not have the security of a long suit. Against that, South has pre-empted the bidding, so you will be unlucky to concede a penalty.

(c)
♠ KQ107
♡ 52
◇ A6
♣ A10986

You are showing at least an opening bid and length in the two suits not mentioned by the opposition.

(d)   ♠ AK108
                                       ♡ AJ97
                                       ◇ 4
                                       ♣ Q1086

A sound opener, with length in the other suits, particularly the majors. Your action has committed the partnership to at least a two-level contract, so you require a better hand than in (a).

Remember, all the above are takeout doubles, because *your partner has not made a positive call* **and** *it is your first turn to speak.* After that, doubles revert to their normal function of penalty seeking.

Pushing the Opponents Around

Now we look at those times when you wish to be involved, but more in the role of a 'thorn in the side' of your opponents. The examples below type-cast that role:

(a) *North/South Game. Dealer East.*

West	North	East	South
–	–	Pass	1◇
?			

West holds:

                                       ♠ KJ9753
                                       ♡ 73
                                       ◇ 64
                                       ♣ K108

(h) *Love All. Dealer South.*

West	North	East	South
–	–	–	1◇
?			

West holds:

                                       ♠ 73
                                       ♡ AQJ10864
                                       ◇ 7
                                       ♣ 753

(c) *East/West Game. Dealer South.*

West	North	East	South
–	–	–	1♠
?			

West holds:

♠ 73
♡ KJ9753
◊ 64
♣ K108

In (a), you hold a meagre 7 points and a not terribly inspiring six card suit. Nevertheless, I would strongly advise a 1♠ overcall. It will inconvenience North every time he wishes to respond in hearts and it may enable your partner to get involved by raising spades.

You are not trying to reach a high-level contract, but at this early stage only you know that. *Your* objective is to make life uncomfortable for your opponents and to force them to guess more often. Like all of us, they will guess wrongly enough times to justify the occasional loss incurred by poking your nose in. *Never be an easy opponent.*

In (b) we have the opportunity to go even higher and cause even more disruption. On a hand like this one which you would have opened with a pre-emptive three level bid, it is quite sound to overcall at a similar level. Be careful, though, because a pre-emptive overcall is not as valuable a tool as an opening. One opponent has already gone some way to describing his hand, making it easier for his partner to judge correctly.

Nevertheless, with a good seven card suit, and little defence, this hand is an ideal 3♡ overcall. Just look at this lay-out and you will see how difficult the bid can be to cope with:

Love All. Dealer South.

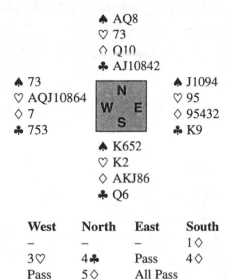

♠ AQ8
♡ 73
◇ Q10
♣ AJ10842

♠ 73
♡ AQJ10864
◇ 7
♣ 753

♠ J1094
♡ 95
◇ 95432
♣ K9

♠ K652
♡ K2
◇ AKJ86
♣ Q6

West	North	East	South
–	–	–	1◇
3♡	4♣	Pass	4◇
Pass	5◇	All Pass	

Your 3♡ bid forced North into bidding at the four level, thus by-passing the only making game – 3NT. Against any other contract the defence will win at least two hearts and ♣K, so whether North/South arrived in 4♠, 5♣ or 5◇ was immaterial. Your pre-emptive bid created a good result without the opponents doing anything foolish.

In (c), the odds are not so neatly stacked in our favour. First, despite a having similar hand to (a), we cannot overcall at the one level. With a minimum hand, a two-level bid is risky because you are advertising a stronger hand, i.e. you are trying to make eight tricks. Partner may take you more seriously and the opposition are more liable to double you, realising their potential reward is greater.

Second, you are vulnerable. The vulnerability of the hand is most critical when judging any competitive action (see 'Sacrificing' later). This is because any overcall provides an opponent with two distinct choices, either bid on and try to play the hand, or pass/double and defend. If the vulnerability favours either decision, that may tip the balance.

The following table should give you some idea of how vulnerability affects marginal decisions:

| THEY | NOT VULNERABLE | VULNERABLE |
WE ↓ →		
NOT VULNERABLE	PLAY	PLAY, but quite close
VULNERABLE	DEFEND, but quite close	DEFEND

So be very wary about vulnerable two-level overcalls, and try to keep them to six card suits *and* sound openings. Below we have a couple of solid citizens, i.e. over 1♠ bid 2♡ on:

(a)   ♠ K6
      ♡ AQ10984
      ◊ KJ7
      ♣ 73

(b)   ♠ 6
      ♡ KJ10973
      ◊ AQ42
      ♣ Q7

Lead Directing

As I said in *Improve your Bridge at Home* the opening lead is fraught with problems, and many, many contracts are allowed home simply because of a poor lead. Take example (b), a couple of pages ago. If after pushing the opponents into 5◊, you lead ♡A, all the good work in the bidding will be lost.

One of the few ways, in fact almost the only way, we can help partner's lead is to bid a suit. If he is co-operating (not always a certainty by any means!), then he will often lead that suit against the final contract. Hence, overcalls designed to attract a particular lead do not have to be unduly strong. Here are three typical 'lead directors':

(a) *Love All. Dealer South.*

West	North	East	South
–	–	–	1♣
?			

West holds:

      ♠ 73
      ♡ 753
      ◊ KQ1094
      ♣ Q108

(b) *North/South Game. Dealer East.*

West	North	East	South
–	–	Pass	1 ◇
?			

West holds:

> ♠ AK1094
> ♡ 732
> ◇ 73
> ♣ 654

(c) *Love All. Dealer East.*

West	North	East	South
–	–	Pass	1 ◇
?			

West holds:

> ♠ Q9532
> ♡ KJ7
> ◇ Q8
> ♣ Q94

On (a), overcall 1 ◇ because, if you do not mention diamonds now, you will almost certainly never have another chance. The odds are in favour of North responding in a major suit, being supported and eventually playing the hand. In that event, you are very keen that partner leads diamonds and not a suit 'of his fancy'. To overcall is the best way of ensuring that you get what you want.

On (b), overcall 1 ♠, same principle as (a) above. Here you gain another slight advantage in that North cannot respond 1 ♡. Of course, such an overcall could go wrong, particularly if North doubles, but the risk is worth taking to ensure that East starts the defence with a spade.

On (c), pass. There is little chance that your side will declare the contract as you are facing a 'passed partner', and hold a fairly ordinary 10 point hand. Furthermore, your holdings in hearts and clubs will provide adequate 'support' should partner care to lead one. There is no need to direct his lead if you are happy with anything. Pass and leave it to him. You never know, something devastating may appear!

Taking up Bidding Space

We saw earlier how a 3♡ pre-emptive overcall caused insurmountable problems for the opponents. Why did that happen? The primary reason was that they were denied 'bidding space'. Space is your friend when you are bidding, guard it jealously. If you use it frugally, you will find that many tricky problem hands can be taken care of without undue guesswork.

However, it is also your job to deny the opposition space, and make their life difficult. I repeat:

'Never be an Easy Opponent'.

So, when you have the chance to make a nuisance of yourself, take it. We will look at three examples on this theme:

(a) *Love All. Dealer East.*

West	North	East	South
–	–	Pass	1♣
?			

West holds:

> ♠ KJ984
> ♡ 7
> ◊ Q1086
> ♣ J84

(b) *North/South Game. Dealer North.*

West	North	East	South
–	Pass	Pass	1◊
?			

West holds:

> ♠73
> ♡ 864
> ◊ 73
> ♣ AKJ1084

(c) *North/South Game. Dealer East.*

West	North	East	South
–	–	Pass	1♡
?			

West holds:

♠ KJ943
♡ 7
◊ Q1086
♣ J84

On (a) bid 1♠, thereby 'blocking out' a 1◊ or 1♡ response. Risky, but worth doing, I assure you.

On (b) bid 2♣ (you cannot bid 3♣ pre-emptive, because it is a strong jump overcall: 4♣ would be a pre-empt (double jump)).

On (c) pass. No bidding space is taken up by overcalling 1♠, your suit is not particularly dynamic and you do not expect to play the hand. If that was not enough, there is an excellent chance that you will be on lead in any case (South declaring a heart contract at some level). All in all, you have no good reason to bid.

In a moment we will look from the other side of the table, and develop a sensible strategy for responding effectively. First, a short quiz:

Quiz

1. South opens the bidding with 1◊ at Game All. Sitting West, what if anything would you bid on these hands:

(a)	♠ KQ10864	(b)	♠ A64	(c)	♠ J8432	(d)	♠ J84
	♡ 64		♡ A973		♡ KJ9		♡ KQ1097
	◊ A83		◊ J84		◊ Q8		◊ J84
	♣ 84		♣ A92		♣ Q94		♣ Q9

2. What would you bid with these hands in the following situation:

Love All. Dealer North.

West	North	East	South
–	1◊	Dble	Pass
?			

(a)	♠ KJ	(b)	♠ Q98653	(c)	♠ Q9	(d)	♠ AJ94
	♡ K9873		♡ KJ		♡ 10864		♡ AQ84
	◊ 10753		◊ 973		◊ J9753		◊ 732
	♣ Q2		♣ AJ		♣ J9		♣ 74

3. What would you bid on the same hands if South had raised to 2◊ i.e.

West	North	East	South
–	1◊	Dble	2◊
?			

4. What would you bid, as West, after this sequence:

Love All. Dealer North.

West	North	East	South
–	1◊	Pass	1♡
?			

(a) ♠ AQJ10864   (b) ♠ QJ97   (c) ♠ Q94   (d) ♠ A64
    ♡ 73   ♡ A73   ♡ J9   ♡ AQ107
    ◊ 7   ◊ 7   ◊ Q108   ◊ KQ10
    ♣ Q108   ♣ AQ1094   ♣ AQJ42   ♣ K84

Answers

1. **(a)** 1♠. For the lead, and also it may be your hand. Remember, an overcall implies that you can take tricks, whereas an opening says you have points.

   (b) Pass. You should almost never overcall a four card suit, even here when you have three aces. You have an opening bid, not an overcall. This hand highlights the difference.

   (c) Pass. A bad suit, vulnerable and only 9 points. Need I say more?

   (d) 1♡. For the lead, but a little risky. If you prefer to pass I, for one, will not argue with you.

2. **(a)** 2♡. Close to 3♡, however. Remember, you bid as if your partner has opened one of your suit.

   (b) 4♠. Easy. Just thrown in for a breather!

   (c) 1♡. Don't be tempted to pass 1◊ doubled with such poor cards in the suit. Partner has announced support for hearts, so there should be nothing to worry about.

(d) 2◇. A cuebid, showing both major suits. Then raise whichever one partner bids to the three level, inviting game.

3. (a) 3♡. To show more than a simple competitive hand, it is necessary to make a jump bid. Your length in diamonds guarantees that partner will have (at most) a singleton, and all your points are in key suits. A fast improving hand.

(b) 4♠. As before.

(c) Pass. There is no need to bid now, so take the opportunity to pass. Doubling 2◇ would be a bad error of judgement.

(d) 3◇. A cuebid as before, except now you have to go to the three level. You have nothing in reserve, so, if partner simply bids a major suit, you should not raise.

4. (a) 3♠. Time to make life difficult, but remember to some extent you have arrived after the boat has sailed. Once the opponents have opened and responded, much of the effect of a pre-empt has been lost. Nevertheless, with such an excellent suit, anything less than 3♠ would be pusillanimous.

(b) Double. A takeout double, showing interest in the unbid suits (here it is spades and clubs) and enough points to enter the auction. The following guidelines should help you determine whether a double is penalty or takeout:

(i) If partner has made any bid (i.e. not a pass) then doubles are penalties.

(ii) All doubles of no trumps are penalties.

(iii) If the opponents have bid three or more suits, double is penalties.

(iv) If you have had a chance to make a double earlier in the sequence, a later double is penalties, for example:

Dealer South.

West	North	East	South
–	–	–	1♡
Pass	1♠	Pass	2♡
Dble			

West's double is penalties, because he could have made a takeout double on the previous round.

(c)   Pass. It would be foolish to enter the bidding with so few playing tricks, and an expectation of weakness in partner's hand.

(d)   1NT. Showing stops in diamonds and hearts. Because the opponents are liable to hold nearly all the remaining points, this overcall must be strong (about 17-19 points is advisable). When only one opponent has bid, for example:

West	North	East	South
–	–	–	1♡
1NT			

This overcall shows about 15-17 points and at least one (good) stop in their suit.

Responding to Overcalls

It is fine for me to say when (and when not) to overcall, but 'what happens next'? How do we construct a sensible dialogue to get to the right contract?

In out-and-out competitive bidding, we should bear one thing firmly in mind: '*Whenever possible, support partner*'. For example:

Game All. Dealer North.

West	North	East	South
–	1◇	1♠	2♣
?			

West holds:

♠ Q94
♡ KJ985
◇ Q42
♣ 73

Bid 2♠ (not 2♡). A fit *might* exist in hearts, but in trying to find out if it does, you will miss a golden chance to tell your partner that a fit *does* exist in spades. When the bidding is competitive, as it is here, that is *the* most useful piece of information you can put across.

How do we develop the bidding if partner overcalls and we have a good hand? Consider ths situation:

East/West Game. Dealer North.

West	North	East	South
–	1◇	1♠	Pass
?			

What would you bid, as West, with:

(a) ♠ A7	(b) ♠ 7	(c) ♠ QJ84	(d) ♠ Q108
♡ 1084	♡ AQ10984	♡ AJ9	♡ AJ94
◇ AJ94	◇ K73	◇ 73	◇ 73
♣ Q984	♣ Q94	♣ A1084	♣ A1084

(a) Bid 1NT. This response shows about 9-11 points (usually with less than 9, and lacking support, you will pass 1♠). A jump to 2NT needs about 12-14 points, and 3NT can be bid with 15 or more. The reason for demanding higher point-counts than we would need if responding to a 1♠ opening, is that an overcall can be made on a hand which is too weak to open. We must give partner more licence and hence we need a bit more to get excited.

(b) Bid 2♡. Opinions vary as to whether a 'change of suit' should be forcing or non-forcing, i.e. whether the overcaller *must* bid again or not. I think a non-forcing style allows greater freedom to overcall and I would recommend that to you. With a better hand than this one, for example:

> ♠ 7
> ♡ AQ10984
> ◇ K73
> ♣ AQ4

Bid 3♡

(c) Bid 3♠. You probably would have raised an opening 1♠ to 4♠, but as in (a), we give partner a little more rope when he has overcalled. Bear in mind that if you have overcalled 1♠ with a minimum *opening bid*, you have an *above minimum* overcall. The lowest point count for an acceptable overcall is about eight. Hence with:

> ♠ AK932
> ♡ K73
> ◇ 1084
> ♣ Q2

Bid 4♠ on this sequence:

West	North	East	South
–	1♢	1♠	Pass
3♠	Pass	?	

(d) Bid 2♢. What is often referred to as 'the unassuming cuebid' or UCB. We cuebid the opponents suit in response to an overcall, to tell partner the following:

    (i)   I have at least 10 points.
    (ii)   I do not have a good stop in the opponents' suit.
    (iii) I have reasonable support for your suit.
    (iv) I do not have a good suit of my own.

Put more bluntly, I have a decent hand, but don't know what to do with it!

Replying to a UCB is basically commonsense. For example, what would you bid with these three hands on the sequence as shown:

West	North	East	South
–	1♢	1♠	Pass
2♢	Pass	?	

(a) ♠ KJ984	**(b)** ♠ Q10842	**(c)** ♠ Q10842
♡ AQ7	♡ A7	♡ AQJ7
♢ 73	♢ AJ94	♢ 7
♣ 984	♣ J8	♣ A73

My suggestions are:

(a) Bid 2♠. You have a fairly minimum overcall and no desire to play any higher.

(b) Bid 2NT. With 12 points and good diamonds you can suggest game in either no trumps or spades.

(c) Bid 3♡. With a sound opening bid, you have extra strength. Continue by describing your hand further and leave partner to judge.

We have looked extensively at overcalls and later developments, now it is time to see how we can deal effectively with the 'Invaders'.

Countering an Overcall/Takeout Double

The Opponents Overcall

When partner opens the bidding, one has a 'right' to have an uninterrupted sequence to the final contract. That is what I *wish*, but it does not always happen. Frequently, we are interrupted by an opponent 'butting-in'.

It is important that we do not let that distraction affect our bidding too much, but nevertheless we must take account of it. Here is a typical example:

Love All. Dealer East.

West	North	East	South
–	–	1◇	1♠
?			

West holds:

♠ J32
♡ AQ7
◇ J108
♣ A1094

Without South's intervention, West would have had a relatively easy response of 2NT, showing about 11-12 points and a balanced hand. However, to bid 2NT *now*, with no certain stop in spades, is ostrich-like in the extreme. West must be flexible and try a different approach. How would you tackle the situation?

First, I would suggest West bids 2♣, and if partner responds 2◇ as often happens, West should *then* invite game. That could be done in one of two ways, either:

(a) Raise diamonds

West	North	East	South
–	–	1◇	1♠
2♣	Pass	2◇	Pass
3◇			

or **(b)** 'Cuebid' spades

West	North	East	South
–	–	1◇	1♠
2♣	Pass	2◇	Pass
2♠			

The cuebid of an opponent's suit, *below the level of 3NT*, asks partner to
bid no trumps if he has a stop in that suit. Here East would bid 2NT with:

♠ K74
♡ J8
◇ AKQ94
♣ 532

but 3♣ with:

♠ 974
♡ J8
◇ AKQ94
♣ K32

With extra playing strength and a spade stop, East could jump to 3NT, thus
accepting partner's invitation, for example:

♠ K74
♡ J8
◇ AKQ942
♣ 53

West	North	East	South
–	–	1◇	1♠
2♣	Pass	2◇	Pass
2♠	Pass	3NT	

Do not worry about the absence of a heart stop, partner should be able to
take care of all unbid suits. Here are some other sequences where West is
making a similar cuebid:

(a)

West	North	East	South
–	–	1♣	Pass
1♡	2◇	3♣	Pass
3◇			

(b)

West	North	East	South
–	–	1♣	1◇
1♡	2◇	3♣	Pass
3◇			

Occasionally, an opponent really treads on our toes. Witness:

West	North	East	South
–		1◇	2♣
?			

At Love All, West holds:

♠ A62
♡ Q94
◇ 73
♣ KJ842

West also wanted to bid 2♣, so he must express his indignation by doubling for penalties. Note that because East has made a positive call a double is no longer 'takeout'. Be careful, though, not to be overly trigger-happy.

Test your 'speed on the draw' with a brief Quiz.

Quiz

Love All. Dealer East.

West	North	East	South
–	–	1◇	1♠
?			

Which of these hands do you consider to be worthy of a double of 1♠?

(a) ♠ K842	(b) ♠ Q9532	(c) ♠ KJ94	(d) ♠ Q10842
♡ J73	♡ J73	♡ 1082	♡ AQ106
◇ K42	◇ J73	◇ A6	◇ 7
♣ Q94	♣ Q2	♣ Q1084	♣ AQ4

My vote would be to double on (c) and (d).

(a) is too weak in spades (note the difference that adding ♠J9 makes in (c)), so I would bid 1NT, and (b) is just too weak period. I would *pass.*

The ♠9 in (c) is almost worth an extra trick because you can make a working assumption that ♠AQ10 will be on your right. Also the possession of an ace, and relative shortage in partner's suit all bode well for a penalty.

With (d) we can almost guarantee at least a game contract, but nevertheless I would still double. The compensation is likely to be on a par with a game bonus, and may easily be more. And it satisfies the mean streak in us!

The Opponents Double

A takeout double has not affected the space available, nor has it implied a particular suit. Nevertheless, it must affect how we approach the bidding. There are *three changes to be made*:

1. Raises of partner's suit become more 'defensive' and less constructive.
2. A suit bid by responder is no longer forcing (unless it is a *jump response*).
3. Hands of 10 points or more usually begin with 're-double'.

The idea behind this approach is to give the maximum chance of inflicting a penalty on the opposition, whilst at the same time avoiding one yourself. Here is one example of each principle in action:

1. Raises are More 'Defensive'
East/West Game. Dealer South.

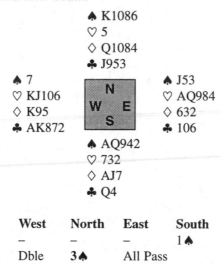

	♠ K1086	
	♡ 5	
	◊ Q1084	
	♣ J953	

♠ 7   ♠ J53
♡ KJ106   ♡ AQ984
◊ K95   ◊ 632
♣ AK872   ♣ 106

♠ AQ942
♡ 732
◊ AJ7
♣ Q4

West	North	East	South
–	–	–	1♠
Dble	3♠	All Pass	

North's defensive 3♠ bid effectively silences East, who is dying to mention his hearts. Had North only raised to 2♠, East would have been able to enter the auction with 3♡, leading to East/West reaching a makeable 4♡ contract.

2. A New Suit is Not Forcing

As both 'redouble' and a jump response are available to handle our better hands, we have the opportunity to bid suits while not showing particular strength. It is important to make use of this facility, for example:

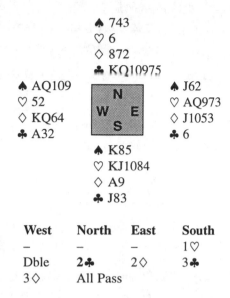

♠ 743
♡ 6
◇ 872
♣ KQ10975

♠ AQ109
♡ 52
◇ KQ64
♣ A32

♠ J62
♡ AQ973
◇ J1053
♣ 6

♠ K85
♡ KJ1084
◇ A9
♣ J83

West	North	East	South
–	–	–	1♡
Dble	2♣	2◇	3♣
3◇	All Pass		

North has the chance to bid his clubs which is valuable for three reasons:

(i) It could help his partner with the opening lead and later defence.
(ii) It may enable his side to successfully compete the bidding.
(iii) It may avoid a nasty penalty.

To underline **(iii)** just consider the hand above, should North pass:

West	North	East	South
–	–	–	1♡
Dble	**Pass**	Pass	Pass

South must declare 1♡ doubled, and it will not be a happy experience for him. He will lose (at least) 3 spades, 1 diamond, 1 heart and 1 club on top, plus two club ruffs and maybe ♡Q as well. A disastrous result. Don't blame South, though, because he had a sound five card suit and nowhere to go.

3. Re-double with 10 Points or More
What happens after our multi-purpose re-double? We have announced that our side has the greater strength, and we are on the warpath. Now, all doubles are penalties, and 'new' suit bids by the re-doubler are forcing for one round (i.e. opener must not pass, otherwise he will lose £200, and a partner!). Let us see how this works in practice:

East/West Game. Dealer South.

West	North	East	South
–	–	–	1♡
Dble	Rdbl	1♠	Pass
Pass	?		

You are North, how would you handle these hands:

(a) ♠ K94	(b) ♠ KJ94	(c) ♠ K94	(d) ♠ 64
♡ J73	♡ A6	♡ J6	♡ A73
◇ KQ84	◇ Q1084	◇ AQ1094	◇ AQ84
♣ Q43	♣ Q32	♣ K63	♣ K763

I suggest the following:

(a) 1NT. Although 11 points is normally enough to bid 2NT, here there is no need to raise the level. Having already shown at least 10 points, 1NT can be reserved for 10 and 11 point hands, leaving 2NT for 12 points (or a 'good' 11 such as ♠K108, ♡J107, ◇KQ104, and ♣Q93).

(b) Double. Time to punish your vulnerable opponents. They have stepped into the bidding at the wrong time and must pay for their impudence. Incidentally, it is sensible for partner to lead a trump in such circumstances, (i.e. your side has the balance of points), to cut down on the opponents' ability to ruff. You have more assets that can be ruffed away.

(c) 2◇. Natural and *forcing*. With a weaker hand you would have bid immediately over the double, or even passed and 'protected' (see later).

(d) 2♠. A cuebid, announcing a good hand, but with nothing obvious to say. It also states that you have game-going values. Partner should make a descriptive bid which will help you in deciding which contract to play, for example:

(a) ♠ AJ9	(b) ♠ 1083	(c) ♠ 1083
♡ KQ1062	♡ KQ1062	♡ KQ1062
◇ K7	◇ K7	◇ K
♣ 1084	♣ AJ8	♣ AJ84
Bid 2NT	Bid 3♡	Bid 3♣

You can then proceed accordingly, i.e. (a)3NT (b)4♡ (c)4♡.

2
HIGH-LEVEL COMPETITION

One of the hardest skills for a bridge player to acquire is the ability to judge high-level competitive deals accurately. When do we 'sacrifice', when do we double the opponents, and when do we bid 'one for the road'? If I always knew the answers to those questions I would be a happy (and wealthy) man!

There are some principles which will help us decide what to do. Before I begin, let me first show you the kind of deal on which your best calculations can be thrown into disarray – by wild distribution.

East/West Game. Dealer West.

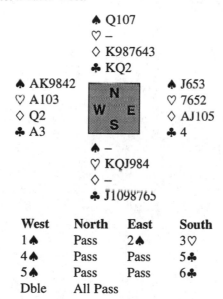

```
                    ♠ Q107
                    ♡ –
                    ◇ K987643
                    ♣ KQ2
      ♠ AK9842                  ♠ J653
      ♡ A103                    ♡ 7652
      ◇ Q2                      ◇ AJ105
      ♣ A3                      ♣ 4
                    ♠ –
                    ♡ KQJ984
                    ◇ –
                    ♣ J1098765
```

West	North	East	South
1♠	Pass	2♠	3♡
4♠	Pass	Pass	5♣
5♠	Pass	Pass	6♣
Dble	All Pass		

East/West have done everything right in this sequence – *in theory*. They have competed to the level (5♠) which they expect to make and, when

South who has adopted a Rambo-style approach to the bidding 'sacrifices' in 6♣, West with three aces confidently doubles.

Amazingly, despite holding all four aces between them, East/West cannot defeat South's slam. Even if West leads ♣A and another club, to cut down on dummy's ability to ruff, South simply enters his hand and leads ♡K planning to discard from dummy if it is not covered by the Ace (*a ruffing finesse*).

When West's ♡A dutifully appears, dummy ruffs with its sole remaining trump. South now returns to hand and cashes ♡Q and ♡J. Of course the ten conveniently arrives on cue and his hand is high. A bizarre result.

However good your judgement may be, such results are bound to happen from time to time; that is the nature of bridge. You just have to shrug your shoulders and chalk it up to experience.

Once that caveat is out of the way, I can return to the principles that will guide you in determining when to bid, double or pass at high level. I am safe in the knowledge that I will not be blamed for every disaster!

In summary, these are as follows:

When to Sacrifice

A 'sacrifice' is a manoeuvre whereby a contract is bid despite expecting it to fail. The motive behind such a tactic is the belief that the resultant penalty (even if doubled) will be less than the value of the opposing contract.

It is essential, for this strategy to work properly, that you only use it when you are sure that you cannot defeat the opposition. Here is an example of the kind of decision you might face:

East/West Game. Dealer North.

West	North	East	South
–	Pass	1♡	1♠
2◇	2♠	4♡	?

South holds:

♠KQ10983
♡10
◇Q4
♣KQ103

You need to consider prospects from two distinct angles:

1. **Defensive:** Do you think that 4♡ is likely to make?

2. **Offensive:** Do you think that 4♠ doubled (as it is almost certain to be) will be relatively inexpensive?

If the answer to both of these questions is 'Yes' then you should sacrifice, i.e. bid 4♠, more as a lion than a lamb to the slaughter. The concept of 'damage limitation', or more accurately loss limitation, is one which is just as important as profit maximisation. No-one can hope to 'win' every hand, but to restrict your losses is absolutely crucial.

On the South hand above, I would consider the following points:

1. Defensive

(a) We have no ace, giving East/West control of most suits.
(b) We have a six card spade suit, reducing the chance of winning any tricks there.
(c) We have ◊Q 'underneath' dummy's diamond suit.
(d) Any trump finesse required by declarer will be 'on-side'.

In other words, our defensive potential is highly limited – probably to one trick in clubs (or two if we are lucky).

2. Offensive

(a) We have a good six card trump suit, giving us security against bad breaks.
(b) We have a solid side suit to tackle, which is likely to bring in extra tricks.
(c) We have only five 'top' losers.

We can expect to do relatively well in 4♠, and eight tricks would be our low prediction, nine our likely result, and ten once in a purple moon.

All in all, we have a fairly clear 4♠ bid.

On the following layout, which is consistent with the bidding, 4♡ will make an overtrick (or two if South leads ♣K) and 4♠ will be one down. North/South will have improved their result from minus 850 (for a vulnerable game and rubber) to minus 100 for a non-vulnerable doubled under-trick. A 'profit' of 750 points on the deal.

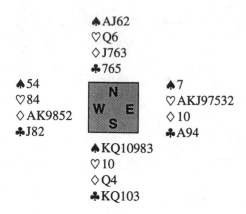

```
              ♠ AJ62
              ♡ Q6
              ◇ J763
              ♣ 765
  ♠ 54                        ♠ 7
  ♡ 84                        ♡ AKJ97532
  ◇ AK9852                    ◇ 10
  ♣ J82                       ♣ A94
              ♠ KQ10983
              ♡ 10
              ◇ Q4
              ♣ KQ103
```

Remember, good bridge tactics involve loss limitation as well as profit maximisation or:

'Take each deal on its own merits.
Do not feel, like many gamblers,
that you have to 'win' every hand.'

When to Double the Opponents

Here is a typical 'push and shove' auction:

North/South Game. Dealer North.

West	North	East	South
–	1♡	1♠	3♡
3♠	4♡	4♠	?

South holds:

```
              ♠ 832
              ♡ KJ94
              ◇ KJ10
              ♣ K73
```

What should he say: pass, double or 5♡?

You must always ask yourself the following questions before taking the plunge:

1.   Is my hand basically offensive or defensive?
2.   Do I have unexpected distribution?

3.   Does my partner know my hand within reasonable bounds?
4.   Do I know my partner's hand within reasonable bounds?
5.   Have we bid constructively or destructively?

A lot to think about, but the answers at least should be brief, i.e. 'yes' or
'no'! Each question needs a little amplification to understand the principle
behind it.

1. Offensive or Defensive?
An offensive hand is not one which shouts abuse at you when you pick it
up. Instead it has *strength in its long suits* with solid holdings such as KQs
or QJs.

Here are three South hands which could have bid 3♡ in the above
sequence: are they offensive, defensive, or neutral?

(a) ♠ Q74	(b) ♠ 432	(c) ♠ 1096
♡ Q1084	♡ KJ109	♡ K543
◇ KJ102	◇ KQJ4	◇ QJ107
♣ Q8	♣ 86	♣ KJ

I would vote:

(a) Defensive   (b) Offensive   (c) Neutral
                                      (◇ = offensive
                                       ♣ = defensive)

Obviously, if your hand is basically offensive, you should tend to bid, if
defensive 'double', and neutral 'pass'. Our actual hand is neutral in my
opinion, but I wouldn't argue if you said it had defensive tendencies.

2. Unexpected Distribution?
Again, I will refer to the example sequence to give an idea of what we are
looking for. A raise to 3♡ would usually be a fairly balanced hand, four
hearts and about 11 points or so. Hence, any of the following would fall
outside the norm, as they possess fewer high card points with
distributional values as compensation:

(a) ♠ 7	(b) ♠ 876	(c) ♠ 653
♡ J10842	♡ Q1084	♡ J10862
◇ AQ942	◇ AJ984	◇ —
♣ 73	♣ 7	♣ AJ1093

Any similar hand will tend to bid because partner cannot possibly judge accurately what we have. Thus he cannot be expected to make the winning decision, so 'take charge' and bid 5♡.

3. Is My Hand Known?

In our example sequence as South, we have had the opportunity to make a limit bid of 3♡, thus defining our hand within reasonable bounds. Sometimes life is not so kind to us, for example:

Love All. Dealer South.

West	North	East	South
–	–	–	Pass
1♣	4♠	5♣	?

All North knows about the South hand can be written on a postage stamp, i.e. it has less than opening values. The onus is now on *South* to decide whether to pass, double or bid 5♠. Here are three candidates:

(a)	♠ Q108	(b)	♠ 74	(c)	♠ 7
	♡ 7		♡ Q1082		♡ K953
	◇ AJ8753		◇ QJ985		◇ 6543
	♣ 653		♣ 65		♣ QJ108

On (a) you should bid 5♠. Do not be worried about holding three clubs: because it guarantees that your partner is short in the suit, it is *not* a minus feature. Do not be tempted by the argument of some players who pass in this position, saying 'Partner can bid again if he wants to'. That puts too much pressure on partner, for he cannot possibly know if you hold hand (a), (b) or (c). Remember: if you have accurately described your hand, leave the decision to partner and– crucially in this case – the corollary holds true.

On (b), we can pass with a clear conscience, because we have no particular view of what is best; whereas (c) is a clear candidate for a 'double'. True, we cannot *guarantee* to defeat 5♣, but we have a very good chance to do so *and* we will dissuade North from making a second bid on something like:

♠ KQJ10842
♡ 7
◇ AJ987
♣ –

Where he might otherwise have been sorely tempted.

4. Is My Partner's Hand Known?

Let us go all the way back to the 'push and shove'. Here it is again:

North/South Game. Dealer North.

West	North	East	South
–	1♡	1♠	3♡
3♠	4♡	4♠	?

What do we know about the North hand? Consider these three hands below, are they all possible?

(a) ♠ Q	(b) ♠ 5	(c) ♠ 5
♡ AQ1075	♡ AQ1075	♡ AQ10753
◇ KJ32	◇ AQ432	◇ A43
♣ 986	♣ 98	♣ Q108
No	**No**	**Yes**

On (a), North should *pass over* 3♠ for two reasons:

   (i)   He would have passed a direct raise to 3♡, so why bid now?

   (ii) He has limited defence to 4♠, so why push the opponents into it?

On (b), North has the values (in playing tricks) to bid 4♡, but nevertheless should not do so. Here, envisaging a 4♠ enemy call, he should *select* 4◇, bringing his second suit into play. This will help his partner in two ways:

(i)   *By allowing him to judge the 'fit' in North's key side suit,* and hence determine whether to bid on to 5♡ over 4♠.

(ii) *By enabling the defence to 4♠ to be more accurate in alerting South to the concentration of strength (and length) in diamonds.*

Finally, with (c), North will indeed bid 4♡, and thus we have found a 'typical' hand-type. Therefore, we can say that partner's hand is *reasonably* well known, without being defined to the nth degree. In this instance, the onus is on South to make the key decision.

5. Constructive or Destructive?

When we have bid constructively to a contract, we are bidding it to make, rather than to sacrifice. In such situations it can be assumed that our opponents are sacrificing against us. Therefore, we should eliminate the possibility of allowing the opponents to play undoubled. We have two courses of action open to us, either double or bid on.

To illustrate the concept properly, here are three example sequences; on which would you say that North/South have bid *their* contract constructively?

(a)	West	North	East	South
	–	1♡	1♠	2♡
	2♠	3♡	3♠	4♡
	4♠	?		

(b)	West	North	East	South
	–	1♡	1♠	2♣
	2♠	3◇	3♠	4♡
	4♠	?		

(c)	West	North	East	South
	–	1♡	1♠	3♣
	3♠	4♣	4♠	?

Sequence (a) sounds like 'I don't care what the result is, I refuse to miss my turn'. To determine if North/South are forced to act (bid or double), we must untangle their bidding from their opponents and see what conclusions we can draw. A good trick here is to 'cancel' East/West's bidding in your mind and see how North/South have bid 'on their own':

West	North	East	South
–	1♡	–	2♡
–	3♡	–	4♡

As you can see, they have not shown any enthusiasm for reaching game; rather they have been pushed there. They are bidding 'defensively' and should not feel forced into doing anything further. Compare that with:

West	North	East	South
–	1♡	1♠	2♡
2♠	4♡	4♠	?

Here, North has leapt to game and can be assumed to be 'bidding to make'. Hence, it is expected that North/South will take *some* further action.

Sequence (b) is entirely different, because North/South mention more than one suit, and both players have shown strength by bidding 'freely' when pass was an available option for a weaker hand. Again, look at their bidding in isolation:

West	North	East	South
–	1♡	–	2♣
–	3◊	–	4♡

No question about it, they have bid constructively, and East/West are sacrificing. North/South *must* either double 4♠ or bid on.

In sequence (c), North/South are yet to reach game: how does this affect the situation? Normally, there would be no need to continue bidding, but this sequence is not normal. Why?

When South bid 3♣, it was a jump response, showing a strong hand and 'forcing to game'. Hence, North/South have a significant balance of strength and cannot allow the opponents to steal the contract from them without exacting a suitable punishment. Either they must double 4♠ or continue on to a game (or even slam) in clubs. East/West are just making a nuisance of themselves and must not be taken too seriously.

Remember, on *any* occasion that you have shown game-going values, your opponents cannot play a contract undoubled. Your overall strength, even in the absence of good quality trumps, will defeat them, for example:

North/South Game. Dealer North.

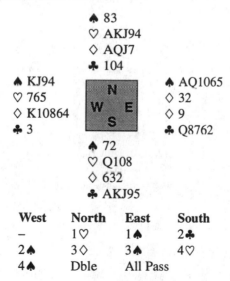

```
                ♠ 83
                ♡ AKJ94
                ◊ AQJ7
                ♣ 104
  ♠ KJ94                      ♠ AQ1065
  ♡ 765          N            ♥ 32
  ◊ K10864    W     E         ◊ 9
  ♣ 3            S            ♣ Q8762
                ♠ 72
                ♡ Q108
                ◊ 632
                ♣ AKJ95
```

West	North	East	South
–	1♡	1♠	2♣
2♠	3◊	3♠	4♡
4♠	Dble	All Pass	

This is sequence (b) in full, with North/South eventually doubling 4♠. Although their trumps are mediocre in the extreme, their balance of strength will easily defeat 4♠ and, by repeatedly leading trumps (always a sound tactic when you have the majority of high cards), they should register a penalty of 300 or 500 points.

Not as good as making 4♡, but that was never an option available to them. They did as well as they reasonably could do. It is never wrong to take sensible compensation, rather than bid on, in pique, and risk a minus score. Take a sure profit rather than an uncertain windfall.

To summarise, here is our 'Five Point Plan':

Question	Yes	No
1. Offensive Hand?	Bid	Pass or Double
2. Unexpected Distribution?	Bid	Pass or Double
3. Hand Known?	Pass	Bid or Double
4. Partner's Hand Known?	Bid or Double	Pass
5. Constructive Bidding?	Bid or Double	Sacrifice or Pass

On our original problem hand (♠832 ♡KJ94 ◇KJ10 ♣K73), we would answer the above questions as follows:

1.	No	Pass/Double
2.	No	Pass/Double
3.	Yes	Pass
4.	Yes (just)	Bid/Double
5.	Yes	Bid/Double

So, we should double 4♠, but to pass would not be a serious error of judgement. A 5♡ bid is not justified.

One for the Road

We have seen one or two examples of decisions to bid on in a competitive sequence. They have a common strand running through them: 'Only bid one more when you have unexpected distribution'. Let me highlight this by returning to two of our previous sequences and adding an entirely new one:

What would you bid in the following situations?

(a) *North/South Game. Dealer North.*

West	North	East	South
–	1♡	1♠	3♡
3♠	4♡	4♠	?

South holds:

♠ 653
♡ J10862
♢ –
♣ AJ1093

(b) *Love All. Dealer South.*

West	North	East	South
–	–	–	Pass
1♣	4♠	5♣	Pass
Pass	?		

North holds:

♠ KQJ10842
♡ 7
♢ AJ987
♣ –

(c) *Love All. Dealer South.*

West	North	East	South
–	–	–	1♡
1♠	3♡	4♠	?

South holds:

♠ –
♡ AQ1096
♢ AQ654
♣ 653

The three hands have certain common characteristics, which can be summarised as:

1. They have not been fully expressed in the bidding to date.

2. They have considerable distribution, making the normal rules regarding high card requirements invalid (see the hand on page 31 for confirmation of this).

3. Partner cannot be expected to judge the situation accurately due to the extreme nature of our hand.

So on (a) we should bid 5♡, (b) 5♢ or 5♠ and (c) 5♡ or 5♢.

The 'either/or' answers reflect the fact that we are attempting to balance two fundamentally different objectives. On the one hand, we have a desire to let partner 'in on our secret', and be involved in the decision-making process by accurately describing our hand. On the other side of the coin, we have a desire not to tell the opponents too much.

To see how these conflicting arguments work in practice, let us return to example (c), and consider two totally different outcomes of the same action:

Love All. Dealer South.

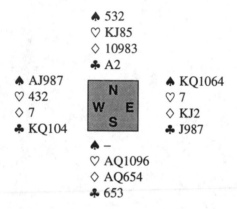

♠ 532
♡ KJ85
◇ 10983
♣ A2

♠ AJ987　　　　♠ KQ1064
♡ 432　　　　　♡ 7
◇ 7　　　　　　◇ KJ2
♣ KQ104　　　　♣ J987

♠ –
♡ AQ1096
◇ AQ654
♣ 653

West	North	East	South
–	–	–	1♡
1♠	3♡	4♠	5◇(i)
5♠(ii)	Dble(iii)	All Pass	

(i)   By bidding 5◇, rather than 5♡, South helps his partner in deciding how to proceed.

(ii) West is listening, and judges that his strength in the black suits justifies a 'save'.

(iii) North has little option but to double holding no 'support' in diamonds.

Five spades doubled is defeated by one trick, North/South scoring 100 points. Had South simply bid 5♡ and not 5◇, it is unlikely that he would have been disturbed. 5♡ would make at least 11 tricks for 450, so by bidding 5◇ 'helpfully' he has achieved a worse result. This time the information was of more value to his opponents.

But, this is not a 'two-headed' coin, as we shall see:

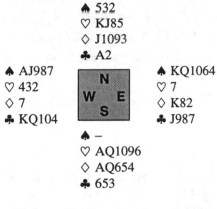

```
                    ♠ 532
                    ♡ KJ85
                    ◇ J1093
                    ♣ A2
      ♠ AJ987                    ♠ KQ1064
      ♡ 432         N            ♡ 7
      ◇ 7        W     E         ◇ K82
      ♣ KQ104       S            ♣ J987
                    ♠ −
                    ♡ AQ1096
                    ◇ AQ654
                    ♣ 653
```

West	North	East	South
–	–	–	1♡
1♠	3♡	4♠	5◇(i)
5♠(ii)	6♡(iii)	All Pass	

(i)   Helpful as before.

(ii) Using his new-found knowledge, as before.

(iii) With better diamonds, ♣A and good heart support
      North can now visualise the perfect fit. He tries
      for a slam.

Now South's picture-painting has drawn a considerable bonus, enabling
his side to reach a making slam on slender values. Without his 5◇ bid,
North would have had no chance of making such an inspired decision.

So which is the right approach? To bid 5◇ helpfully or just 'shut-up-shop'
with 5♡?

The beauty of this game is that no-one can tell. One day a bid will work
perfectly and yet on another day, in exactly the same position, the same
bid will be a disaster. This choice is more a matter of temperament. The
'soloists' will always go for the uncooperative route, whereas those who
like to consult will prefer to paint a picture. You pays your money ....

Before I leave this section, our usual re-cap quiz:

Quiz

1. What is a 'sacrifice'?

2. When should one use the manoeuvre?

3. What do you have to consider when facing a high-level competitive decision?

4. How would you define an 'offensive' hand?

5. Sitting South, what would you bid after the following sequence:

Love All. Dealer East.

West	North	East	South
–	–	1♠	2♡
3♠	4♡	4♠	?

(a) ♠ KJ7
    ♡ AK10952
    ◇ 7
    ♣ QJ4

(b) ♠ J7
    ♡ AKQJ109
    ◇ Q42
    ♣ Q3

(c) ♠ 6542
    ♡ AKJ1094
    ◇ –
    ♣ AQ4

(d) ♠ 6
    ♡ KQ10984
    ◇ KQ1082
    ♣ 6

Answers

1. When you bid a contract, expecting it to fail, but believing the loss will be smaller than allowing the opponents to play their contract.

2. When you have a hand which is offensively strong and defensively weak.

3. (i)   is my hand offensive or defensive?
   (ii) do I have unexpected distribution?
   (iii) do I know my partner's hand?
   (iv) does he know my hand?
   (v)   have we bid constructively or destructively?

4. One which has strength in its long suits.

5. (a) Double (or possibly pass)
   (b) Pass
   (c) 5♡
   (d) 5◇ (or 5♡ for 'soloists')

3
RE-OPENING
AND PROTECTION

Before I leave the 'trenches' and move onto the more peaceful and tranquil area of constructive bidding, I will just mention one or two special situations which may arise, and how to handle them.

There are two concepts I wish to cover, which you will easily guess from the title of the chapter!

Re-openings

A 're-opening' bid is typified by the following situation:

North/South Game. Dealer South.

West	North	East	South
–	–	–	1♢
1♠	Pass	Pass	?

West's intervention of 1♠ has had the effective of silencing North, and East has insufficient strength to respond. In this situation the opener often has a very good hand (15 points or more), and does not wish to give up at the one level. With that sequence in mind, how would you continue (if at all) with the following South hands:

(a) ♠ KJ7 (b) ♠ AQ104 (c) ♠ Q2 (d) ♠ 7
    ♡ J4   ♡ 7   ♡ –   ♡ AQ10
    ♢ AKJ98   ♢ AQ1098   ♢ AKJ984   ♢ KJ987
    ♣ A107   ♣ KJ4   ♣ AQ987   ♣ AQ104

My recommendations are as follows:

(a)   1NT. A re-bid of 1NT opposite a partner who potentially has a complete 'bust', must have more than the usual 15 or 16 points. Here we have 17 points with a solid spade stop and a good suit. About the ideal hand I would say.

(b)   Pass. Any action is liable to result in someone bidding hearts, and that is unlikely to be good news. If your partner bids hearts, you hate it and if an opponent bids hearts they have found a better fit. Just be grateful that West has chosen your second suit and defend tigerishly!

(c)   3♣. You have considerable playing strength and this can only be expressed with a jump re-bid. As little as ♣Kxxx in partner's hand will make game a reasonable bet, and a 2♣ 're-opening' will not fire his enthusiasm. You might bid 2♣ on a hand such as:

♠ Q4
♡ A3
◇ AK1094
♣ KJ108

a completely different animal (more points, less distribution).

(d)   Double. Once more we run across a 'takeout' double, this time defined as a 're-opening' double. It applies when you have opened the bidding and partner has *not* responded.

Here are lots of doubles, which are 're-opening'?

(i)

West	North	East	South
Pass	Pass	1♡	2♣
Dble			

(ii)

West	North	East	South
–	1♡	Pass	2♡
Dble			

(iii)

West	North	East	South
–	Pass	Pass	1♡
Pass	2♡	Pass	Pass
Dble			

(iv)

West	North	East	South
1◇	1♠	Pass	2♠
Dble			

(v)

West	North	East	South
–	1♡	Pass	Pass
Dble			

(vi)	West	North	East	South
	–	–	–	1♡
	Dble	2♡	Pass	Pass
	Dble			

(vii)	West	North	East	South
	1♣	1NT	Pass	Pass
	Dble			

(viii)	West	North	East	South
	1♣	1♠	Pass	Pass
	Dble	2♢	Pass	Pass
	Dble			

(ix)	West	North	East	South
	1♢	Pass	Pass	1♡
	Dble			

I would ascribe the following meanings to West's doubles (in bold type for clarification):

(i) Penalty. West has clubs over South.

(ii) Takeout. South's raise does not affect the meaning of the double as it is West's first turn to bid opposite a passed partner.

(iii) Penalty. With a takeout double, West would have bid on the *first* round.

(iv) Re-opening. West has a good hand with shortage in spades and wishes to hear East's best suit. A typical West hand would be:

$$\spadesuit\ 6$$
$$\heartsuit\ AKJ$$
$$\diamondsuit\ AQ1098$$
$$\clubsuit\ K986$$

(v) Re-opening. The classical situation, where West is short in hearts (also see under 'Protection')

(vi) Re-opening. Although East cannot bid freely over North's heart raise, West still has enough strength to 'drag' a bid out of him. This second double shows something akin to:

♠AQ108
♡8
◇AJ94
♣AJ87

(vii) Penalty. All doubles of no trump contracts are best played as penalties.

(viii) Penalty. West's initial double was 're-opening', showing length in the two unbid suits. Now North has dared to venture into enemy territory and West is showing suitable indignation.

(ix) Re-opening. A small variation on the classical situation.

I have given more than the usual number of examples, because it is crucial to have a sound understanding of when a double is 'takeout' and when it is 'penalty'. If you never go wrong in this area, you will have done better than me!

Protection

Let us return to (v) above (repeated for convenience):

West	North	East	South
–	1♡	Pass	Pass
Dble			

West's double is for takeout, but is also called 'protective'. The idea behind protecting is that your side is likely to have the balance of points because the *opener's partner has passed at his first turn.*

The average expectation would be for opener to hold about 14 points, and his partner about 4. That gives your side approximately 22 points and you should not be defending tamely at the one level in such circumstances. The fact that West may not have the values for a bid directly over the opener, should not debar him from bidding now. For example, these three hands, despite being short of the values to bid directly, are perfectly acceptable 'protective doubles' of 1♡:

(a)	♠ AQ107	(b)	♠ KQ84	(c)	♠ KJ107
	♡ 97		♡ 10		♡ 4
	◇ KJ97		◇ KJ7		◇ KJ87
	♣ 1098		♣ Q10842		♣ J1086

Responder must be careful not to get carried away opposite such a double, because *the doubler has already assumed that he holds a reasonable hand.*

Hence, bid 'one less' opposite a protective double than you would over a direct double, for example:

(a) ♠ KJ108	(b) ♠ KJ9	(c) ♠ Q42
♡ Q1094	♡ Q1082	♡ AJ962
◇ K4	◇ KJ2	◇ K2
♣ J74	♣ K73	♣ K108

(i) In response to a protective double:

Bid 1♠	Bid 2NT	Pass

(ii) In response to a direct double:

Bid 2♠	Bid 3NT	Bid 3NT

The reason for the wide divergence on (c) is due to the fact that we are 'over' declarer's hearts in one case, and 'under' in the other. It is extremely difficult to defend profitably in the latter case (all declarer's trump finesses are 'right').

There is one other protective bid which has a different range – 1NT

West	North	East	South
–	1◇	Pass	Pass
1NT			

Again, because East/West are favourites to have the greater share of the points, 1NT is an attempt to ensure that they will not be cheated out of a contract. Instead of the standard 15-18 points required for East to overcall 1NT, West's bid shows 12-15 points (rather like a 1NT opening) and of course, at least one diamond stop. East should respond appropriately.

That concludes the section on Competitive Bidding, except for a brief quiz on 'Re-openings & Protection'.

Quiz

1. What is the purpose of 're-opening' the bidding?

2. Is the following double 're-opening' or 'penalty'?

West	North	East	South
–	Pass	Pass	1 ◇
Pass	1 ♡	Pass	Pass
Dble			

3. When is a bid 'protective'?

4. How should we respond to a protective double?

5. What is the strength of West's 1NT bid in this sequence:

West	North	East	South
–	1 ◇	Pass	1 ♡
1NT			

Answers

1. When opener has a strong hand and does not wish the opponents to 'buy' the contract at the current level.

2. 'Re-opening'. It does not make sense that West can have a penalty double of 1 ♡ when he does not have enough strength to overcall 1 ♡ earlier. Also, he is 'under' North's suit. West would typically hold something akin to:

   ♠ AJ107
   ♡ 72
   ◇ AQ42
   ♣ Q108

3. When you are in fourth seat, your left hand opponent opens, partner and right hand opponent pass, i.e.:

West	North	East	South
–	1 Plum	Pass	Pass
?			

4. You generally bid a level lower than you would have done over a direct double.

5. 16-19. This is not protection, because South has responded. West needs a strong hand to enter the bidding.

4
SLAM BIDDING

'I never want any of you to bid a slam again!'

Such were the exasperated words of the Captain of a Junior Team I once played in. Having seen many a slam come and go during a Championship, our dearly beloved Captain had reached breaking point.

Junior players do tend to suffer from an excess of *joie de vivre* which is often a fatal flaw when reaching for the skies. Whilst it is possible to 'get away' with a slight paucity of values in lower level contracts, it is not so easy when we can afford to lose at most one trick. Bidding slams is an exciting and thrilling part of the game, however, so it is hardly surprising that we are all keen to do it.

The above serves as a warning: *Do not overbid in the slam zone*. The advice is partly borne out of personal experience and partly out of common sense. After all, in attempting a slam you risk losing a certain game contract and the bonus that goes with it.

It is considered almost greedy not to accept your luck in being dealt a sure game. No one sympathises (least of all partner!) if you bid a slam, fail, and as a consequence lose a rubber that you could have already sewn up.

I hope I haven't put you off bidding slams for ever, because that is certainly not my intention. However, I do believe that in any marginal situation caution should prevail.

There are two types of slam, one based solely on high card strength (these are often declared in no trumps), and the other based on an excellent trump fit and quick tricks in the side suits. Let me first cover no trump slams because it is easier to define when they should be bid.

• • • • •

Slams in No Trumps

To bid a slam your partnership needs considerably over and above the values for game, but how far over? My advice is to bid no trump slams when you can *guarantee at least 34 points between the two hands*. This will limit your opponents to, at most, an ace and a queen or two kings.

Let us see how this rule might work in practice:

1. North/South Game. Dealer South.

♠ KQ4
♡ K108
◇ A742
♣ Q98

♠ AJ108
♡ AQJ
◇ K108
♣ AJ2

West	North	East	South
–	–	–	2NT
Pass	6NT	All Pass	

South opens 2NT, showing between 20 and 22 points. With 14 points, North can visualise a slam and with a balanced hand himself goes straight to the final contract. Despite their overall combined strength, the slam is far from certain to make. Declarer has four spades, three hearts, two diamonds and a club on top and will need some luck in the minor suits to come home.

The reason for this difficulty is one which frequently occurs and on this occasion manifests itself in the heart suit. North/South have 'wasted' a point because, despite the fact that they possess ♡AKQ and J, only three tricks are available.

Change North's hand slightly and a different picture emerges:

♠ KQ4
♡ K1082
◊ A74
♣ Q98

♠ AJ108
♡ AQJ
◊ K108
♣ AJ2

Now South has eleven 'top' tricks and can easily develop the extra one he requires (in clubs). A routine slam, if such a thing exists. We can readily see the potential danger of holdings such as South's hearts, i.e. honours without length, and must bid accordingly. Whenever you hold honours with no extra cards, beware!

Conversely, we can borrow a point or upgrade our hand, when we possess a five card suit as in this example:

Love All. Dealer South.

♠ QJ4
♡ Q108
◊ AQ1084
♣ K6

♠ AK3
♡ K74
◊ K73
♣ AQ82

West	North	East	South
–	–	–	1♣
Pass	1◊	Pass	3NT
Pass	6NT	All Pass	

South's rebid of 3NT shows 19 points, so North knows that he is theoretically one point 'light' for a slam. However, this time he has a five card suit, and it duly supplies the crucial extra trick. With three spades, one heart, five diamonds and three clubs, declarer can even overcome the wastage in spades. Without the 'long' diamond, a slam would have needed quite a little luck.

We can take this principle a little further, within the scope of 'no trump' slams, to when we possess a *good* six card suit. Then we can reduce our points requirement to 31, provided that we have only top cards (aces, kings and queens) outside our main suits. For example:

Love All. Dealer South.

♠ A73
♥ K4
♦ AQJ984
♣ 73

♠ KQ4
♥ A63
♦ K6
♣ AJ1084

West	North	East	South
–	–	–	1♣
Pass	1♦	Pass	2NT
Pass	6NT	All Pass	

South shows 17 or 18 points with his 2NT rebid and although North must assume the lower end (as this is more frequent), he can upgrade his hand because of his six card suit and outside top cards. In practice, 6NT is a simple task for declarer with 12 top tricks.

Slam in Suits

When should we choose to play a slam in a suit rather than in no trumps? The same principles which we saw for selecting a game contract (suit or no trumps) apply with equal force.

To benefit from having a trump suit, we must develop extra tricks by means of either (i) suit establishment, or (ii) ruffing.

To see (i) in action, we will return to our last example, and change the South hand:

♠ A73
♡ K4
◇ AQJ984
♣ 73

♠ J98
♡ AJ3
◇ K10
♣ AKJ84

Again, North/South arrive in 6NT, and prospects are still pretty good. On anything but a spade lead, the contract will almost certainly make and even a spade reduces the chance of success to, at worst, 50%. So why am I repeating this hand? Simply because 6◇ is a much better contract than 6NT, due to our ability to establish a long trick in clubs.

We can use entries to the South hand in diamonds and hearts, to first ruff out as many clubs as required and then reach South to cash the balance (on which North pitches a losing spade or two).

It is time to move onto *more distributional hands*, and the 'when' and 'how' to bid slams. We need to bear in mind the following principles:

1.   We require an outstanding trump fit.

2.   We require 'control' of every suit.

3.   We require either (a) shortages in both hands or (b) a suit to establish or cash.

Our requirement of 34 points to bid a slam is out of the window, because distribution, as we know, is capable of making tricks from low cards almost as easily as high ones.

The 'how' to reach a slam boils down to following one of three basic approaches:

(i)   'Blast' them, leaving everyone in the dark – the non-scientific way.

(ii) 'Cuebid' to ensure that all suits are properly controlled.

(iii) Use 'conventions' to determine the number of aces and kings held.

Let us look at a few hands and see how we might tackle our 'slam hunt'.

East/West Game. Dealer North.

♠ QJ9
♡ J872
◇ AJ4
♣ K108

♠ K4
♡ AKQ1094
◇ KQ103
♣ J

West	North	East	South
–	1NT	Pass	3♡
Pass	4♡	Pass	?

How should South proceed? We can see that a slam is destined to fail because two aces are missing, but North could just as easily hold:

♠ A1086
♡ J87
◇ AJ7
♣ A43

when 7♡ would be a simple contract. Can South find out about how many Aces North has? We introduce our first (and almost last!) convention – that of *Blackwood,* named after its inventor the American, Easley Blackwood. The convention states that:

'When a trump suit has been agreed, a bid of 4NT by either player is artificial and asks his partner how many aces he holds.'

Partner responds in the following way:

5♣	–	0 (or very, very exceptionally, all four)
5◇	–	1
5♡		2
5♠	–	3

After the ace enquiry, a continuation of 5NT asks for kings, the replies being the same, only one level higher:

6♣	–	0 (or all 4)
6◇	–	1
6♡	–	2
6♠	–	3

When you bid 5NT, it guarantees that all the aces are held, otherwise why would you be interested in a grand slam?

Please note that it is highly inadvisable to use Blackwood without an ace, so in effect the 5♣ reply always denies one.

On our example hand, South has his answer to the problem of how to proceed over 4♡, he uses 4NT. Let us see how the story ends:

East/West Game. Dealer North.

♠ QJ9
♡ J872
◇ AJ4
♣ K108

♠ K4
♡ AKQ1094
◇ KQ103
♣ J

West	North	East	South
–	1NT	Pass	3♡
Pass	4♡	Pass	4NT(i)
Pass	5◇(ii)	Pass	5♡(iii)
Pass	Pass(iv)	Pass	

(i)   Blackwood.
(ii) One ace.
(iii) Not enough I'm afraid.
(iv) Sorry, it's all I had!

When the player using Blackwood fails to bid 5NT, he is 'signing-off'. He may sign-off (in this case) in 5♡, 6♡ or 7♡, it doesn't matter. The responder to Blackwood has no right to continue bidding – his partner is in control.

With our 'other' example North hand, South would find his partner's reply to 4NT to be much more to his liking.

East/West Game. Dealer North.

♠ A1086
♡ J87
◊ AJ7
♣ A43

```
      N
   W     E
      S
```

♠ K4
♡ AKQ1094
◊ KQ103
♣ J

West	North	East	South
–	1NT	Pass	3♡
Pass	4♡	Pass	4NT(i)
Pass	5♠(ii)	Pass	7♡(iii)
Pass	Pass(iv)	Pass	

(i)   Our old friend, the 'old Black' (magic?).
(ii) Three aces.
(iii) Thanks, just what I was looking for.
(iv) Good Luck!

A few words of caution about using Blackwood. It is great fun, but do not get carried away. It should be avoided unless:

1.   You are sure that your partnership has the required strength for a slam.

2.   You have an agreed trump suit, one which has been bid *and supported.*

3.   *All* you need to know is the *number* of aces and kings partner holds.

I emphasised 'number', because there is another crucial element to consider, the *location* of aces. To see why, look at this bidding problem:

Love All. Dealer South.

West	North	East	South
–	–	–	1♠
Pass	3♠	Pass	?

South holds:

♠ AKQ1094
♡ 7
◇ 83
♣ AKJ4

How should South proceed?

Blackwood would work perfectly if North has either two aces (bid a slam) or maybe zero (sign off in 5♠). Except in the case of zero when you have three top losers, for example:

♠ J876
♡ KQ42
◇ Q9
♣ Q106

When North has one ace the question is, which one? Using Blackwood will not help us because we need partner to *cooperate* in the investigation of a slam. We use *'cuebidding'* to achieve that.

We cuebid when:

1.   A trump suit has been agreed (as with Blackwood).
2.   We need control of specific suits, rather than any suit

What is a Cuebid?

In essence it *tells partner about the aces we possess*, rather than simply ask about his. In reply partner will show *where* his aces are located, but only if he is willing to go 'slamming'. Thus you also find out partner's opinion as to the prospects of making a slam. A 'double-slammy'.

Returning to South's problem above, we 'cuebid' 4♣ which serves three purposes:

1. It tells North that we have ♣A (or exceptionally a void).
2. It asks North to cuebid any aces he may hold.
3. It asks North's opinion about the quality of his hand, given the bidding to date (i.e. in this case he has shown an invitational raise in spades, about 10-12 points with four card support for spades).

Time to leave the South chair and to concentrate on how North should react to South's 4♣ cuebid.

Love All. Dealer South.

West	North	East	South
–	–	–	1♠
Pass	3♠	Pass	4♣
Pass	?		

How would you continue, as North if you held:

(a) ♠J876	(b) ♠J876	(c) ♠J8765	(d) ♠J876
♡AJ4	♡KQ4	♡AQJ	♡10942
◇QJ5	◇KQ109	◇109	◇AK4
♣1084	♣52	♣Q92	♣Q6

I recommend:

(a) 4♠. Although you have an ace, your hand is very weak in the context of a raise to 3♠, and it is prudent to sign off. Remember, if partner only required one ace, and little more, to go for a slam he would have used Blackwood. Once South has cuebid, *you are involved in the decision-making process*, and should vote accordingly.

(b) 5♠. A maximum hand with second round control in both red suits. You could simply sign-off with 4♠, but your hand has great potential. A bid of 5♠ expresses that perfectly: no aces (otherwise you would bid 4◇ or 4♡), but a super hand otherwise. Opposite:

> ♠ AK10942
> ♡ 73
> ◇ AJ4
> ♣ A4

there is an easy slam, which South should be able to bid with confidence!

(c) 4♡. You were happy to raise 1♠ to 3♠, so there is no reason to deny having ♡A now. On the actual hand, South will sign-off in 4♠, because neither member of the partnership has control of diamonds.

(d) 4♡. As with (c) above, we cuebid in diamonds, but in this instance we find our way to 6♠ as follows:

♠J876
♡10942
◇AK4
♣Q6

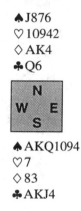

♠AKQ1094
♡7
◇83
♣AKJ4

West	North	East	South
–	–	–	1♠
Pass	3♠	Pass	4♣(i)
Pass	4◇(i)	Pass	6♠(ii)
All Pass			

(i) Cuebids.
(ii) Just what I wanted to hear.

There are occasions when all this science is too much for us, and we feel in the mood for a good, old-fashioned 'punt'. Suppose South held this hand:

♠ AQJ10842
♡ –
◇ 73
♣ AKJ4

and the bidding began as before:

Love All. Dealer South.

West	North	East	South
–	–	–	1♠
Pass	3♠	Pass	?

If South was in a scientific frame of mind, he has a clear 4♣ cuebid. However, he may just fancy a 'pot' at a slam, and leave West to guess what to lead. He would score a big success on this layout:

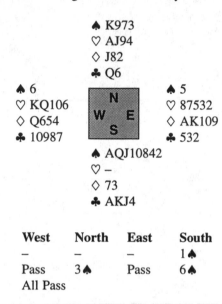

```
              ♠ K973
              ♡ AJ94
              ◊ J82
              ♣ Q6
♠ 6                        ♠ 5
♡ KQ106      N             ♡ 87532
◊ Q654     W   E           ◊ AK109
♣ 10987      S             ♣ 532
              ♠ AQJ10842
              ♡ –
              ◊ 73
              ♣ AKJ4
```

West	North	East	South
–	–	–	1♠
Pass	3♠	Pass	6♠
All Pass			

When West, without the ability to see round corners, would almost certainly lead ♡K allowing the slam home. However, on the other side of the coin, we have:

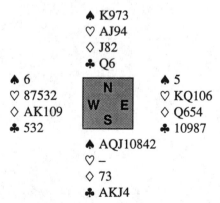

```
              ♠ K973
              ♡ AJ94
              ◊ J82
              ♣ Q6
♠ 6                        ♠ 5
♡ 87532      N             ♡ KQ106
◊ AK109    W   E           ◊ Q654
♣ 532        S             ♣ 10987
              ♠ AQJ10842
              ♡ –
              ◊ 73
              ♣ AKJ4
```

When West would take the first two tricks.

Which approach should you follow? It is a matter of temperament and how much of a gambler you are. However, please note that you need an understanding partner when such a manoeuvre falls flat on its face!

The following is a good test to apply before heading off in a slamwards direction:

> *If you can take an ace from your hand and still be confident of making a game contract, then you have enough to instigate a slam exploration.*

If not, you should play it safe.

Finally, more matches are lost, tournaments thrown away and money discarded by finding hopeless slams which go down, than are won by bidding brilliant slams on marginal values which make. Be warned.

Before we leave slams, a little Quiz.

Quiz

1. What is Blackwood, and when should you use it?

2. What is a cuebid?

3. Should you be cautious or aggressive in the slam zone?

4. How many points do you need for a no trump slam?

5. When do you play a slam in a suit rather than in no trumps?

6. What is 'control' of a suit?

7. What would you bid with the following West hands:

Game All. Dealer West.

West	North	East	South
1♡	1♠	4♡	Pass
?			

West holds:

(a) ♠ A
♡ KQ10987
◊ AK42
♣ 73

(b) ♠ 7
♡ AK1098
◊ KQ1094
♣ K7

(c) ♠ 53
♡ AKQJ7
◊ KQ4
♣ Q93

(d) ♠ A732
♡ AKQ1098
◊ A73
♣ –

Answers

1. Blackwood is a bid of 4NT asking about aces. You should use it only when there is an agreed trump fit, and when you know what to do when you hear the reply.

2. A cuebid is made in a suit to express control (ace or void) of that suit. It is not in any way a natural bid, nor an attempt to play in that suit (trumps must already be clearly established), and carries the following messages:

    (i)   I am interested in a slam, but need your opinion.
    (ii) Blackwood cannot help me at the moment.

3. Cautious. You have more to lose than, for example, when you try for game and fail (where all you risk is a part-score).

4. 34 for a small-slam and 37 for a grand slam (this ensures the opponents cannot have an ace).

5. When you can use trumps to:

    (i)   Establish a side suit.
    (ii) Cross-ruff.

6. Either an ace or a void. A 'second-round control' is a king or singleton, and more sophisticated cuebidding techniques can establish that such controls are present.

7. (a) 4♠. It is best to cuebid the most 'economical' control first. This approach gives partner space to show you whether he has ♣A. If you chose 5◇ instead, East would be unable to bid a slam, even with ♣A, because he would assume you had no control in spades (because you 'missed out' a spade cuebid). Blackwood would be inappropriate, because a 5◇ reply (showing one ace) would leave you unsure as to whether East possessed any club control.

    (b) 4NT Blackwood. The ideal hand for the Convention. Once you know if partner has one, two or three aces, you can select the final contract. If he has no ace, ask him what he was thinking about when he bid 4♡!

(c)   Pass. You have too many gaps to fill. Do not be carried away by
your 17 points or exceptional hearts, but instead concentrate on
what is not there, i.e. ♠AK ♢A and ♣AK. It is almost
inconceivable that East will hold four of these cards. Your hand
is 'balanced', and hence you require 33 points (or so) to make
a slam. That leaves East needing 16, which is not really
possible when he just raised you to game.

(d)   6♡. Any scientific approach is likely to give away more
information than it uncovers. Just 'bash' the slam, leave the
defenders in the dark and trust to Lady Luck!.

Before we leave slam bidding, a last cautionary tale, and a warning about
getting 'carried away':

North/South Game. Dealer South.

West	North	East	South
–	–	–	1♣
Pass	3♣	Pass	?

South held:

♠ KQ
♡ 4
♢ KQ106
♣ AK10987

South was rather an impulsive player, and on seeing an 'ideal' hand for
Blackwood, missing just three aces, he immediately leapt to 4NT. Partner
bid 5♢, dutifully showing his ace, and South suddenly realised something
rather embarrassing. He had to bid 6♣, even though he knew he was
missing two aces! Don't let it happen to you – think carefully before
entering the Slam Zone.

5
THE NATURAL SYSTEM

I have remained true to a very 'natural' system throughout this series but, for ease of reference, I think it is important to gather the various elements 'under one roof'.

I promise not to spring any nasty surprises on you. Think of the next few pages as a 'crib sheet' to be used when you might have forgotten the solution to a particular problem.

We start, as you would expect, with the rules for opening bids.

Opening Bids

1. Opening Bids in Suits

(a) One Level
An opening one-bid in a suit shows approximately 12-20 points and at least four cards in the suit opened. When two or three suits are held, the longest is bid first, and where you have suits of equal length the following rules apply:

2 or more 4 card suits
- open the lowest ranking with up to 16 points
- open the lowest major with 17 or more points

2 five card suits
- open the higher ranking, unless holding clubs and spades when you open 1 ♣.

(b) Two Level
A two-bid shows a strong hand with at least eight playing tricks and at least 17 points. 2 ♣ is reserved for hands of exceptional strength (game forcing) or hands without a suit of quality (including balanced) of 23 points upwards.

(c) Three Level
This is reserved for weak hands with a long suit (seven or more cards) and about six or seven playing tricks, depending on vulnerability.

(d) Four Level
Similar to the three level, except that these bids may hold much greater playing strength. Four level openings have a wider range than their three level counterparts.

2. No Trump Openings

(a) 1NT
Shows between 12 and 14 points and an essentially balanced hand (4-3-3-3, 4-4-3-2, or 5-3-3-2 with a poor five card suit). The ability to open 1NT has *pre-eminence over a suit bid.*

(b) 2NT
A strong balanced hand with 20-22 points.

(c) 3NT
Even stronger – 25-26 points.

Having dealt with opening bids, we move on to *how to respond.*

Responses

1. Responses to 'One of a Suit'

(a) One Level
A simple 'change of suit' at the one level guarantees a minimum of 6 points and has a maximum of 15 points.

(b) Two Level
To make a simple, i.e. non-jump, reply at the two level requires a minimum of 9 points and has the same maximum as before (15). All changes of suit by responder are forcing, i.e. opener cannot pass.

(c) Jump Response
A jump response is defined as a hand with at least 16 points and forces the partnership to (at least) reach a game contract.

(d) Raise of Openers' Suit

    (i) To the Two Level
Shows support for partner's suit (usually four cards or more) and about 6-8 points.

    (ii) To the Three level
As for two level, except 9-11 points.

(iii)   To Game
An opening bid or equivalent strength based on distribution.

(e) No Trumps

(i)   1NT. About 6-9 points and denying the ability to make another call.

(ii)   2NT. About 10-12 points and a balanced hand (nearly always 4-3-3-3 or 4-4-3-2).

(iii)   3NT. A balanced hand of 13-15 points.

2. Responses to Two of a Suit

As a two level opening is forcing, pass is not available as an option for responder, hence bid as follows:

(a)   2NT – *Negative* reply, denying values for a 'positive'.

(b)   New suit (positive) – Shows at least 7 points and a fair quality suit.

(c)   3NT – Shows about 9-11 points and stops outside opener's suit.

(d)   Raise to three level – is a positive reply (seven or more points) with at least three card support.

(e)   Raise to game – less than a positive, with support.

Over a 2♣ opener, 2◇ is the negative and 2NT shows 6-8 points with a balanced hand.

3. Responses to Three of a Suit

A change of suit is forcing and 3NT is to play. A raise of the pre-empt is not an invitation, but a nuisance bid.

4. Responses to No Trump Openings

(a) 1NT

2 of a suit is not forcing, showing less than 11 points and at least a five card suit. Opener is expected to pass.

2NT is invitational, showing about 11 or 12 points and a fairly balanced hand.

3 of a suit is forcing to game, showing at least an opening bid and five or more cards in the suit. Opener is expected to choose between 3NT and game in the suit, depending upon his fit.

All jumps to game are to play, and opener must pass.

(b) 2NT

3 of a suit is forcing (you pass with a weak hand, i.e. less than 4 points) and gives the same message as over 1NT, in that opener decides which game to play.

All bids of game are to play (as before).

(c) 3NT

4♣ and 4◇ are the only forcing bids available, otherwise responder chooses the final contract. The exception is a bid of 4NT which invites opener to bid a slam (usually in no trumps).

Next, we move on to the third bid in the auction.

Continuations by Opener

(a) After a 'One Level' Response
   - (i)   Rebid of 1NT shows 15 or 16 points.
   - (ii)   Rebid of 2NT shows 17 or 18 points.
   - (iii)   Rebid of 3NT shows 19 points.
   - (iv)   Minimum rebid or simple support of responders' suit shows 12-15 points.
   - (v)   Simple change of suit shows 12-17 points.
   - (vi)   A jump raise, jump rebid or 'reverse' (i.e. where the suit rebid is higher ranking than the one opened) shows about 16-18 points.
   - (vii)   A jump in a new suit is forcing to game and shows at least 18 points.

(b) After a 'Two Level' Response
   - (i)   rebid of 2NT shows 15-16 points.
   - (ii)   rebid of 3NT shows 17-19 points.
   - (iii)   Minimum rebid or simple support shows 12-15 points.
   - (iv)   Simple change of suit shows 12-15 points.
   - (v)   Jump raise, jump rebid or 'reverse' shows 16 or more points and are all *forcing to game*.
   - (vi)   Jump in a new suit shows at least 16 points and is also game forcing.

(c) After a 'No Trump' Response
1NT
   - (i)   Pass with any fairly balanced hand and up to 16 points.
   - (ii)   Bid 2NT on 17-18 point balanced hands and 3NT on 19.

(iii)   A two level bid (non-reverse) is just suggesting another contract and shows less than 17 points.

(iv)   A 'reverse', for example 1◇–1NT–2♡, is forcing and shows at least 17 points.

(v)   A jump rebid, for example 1◇–1NT–3◇, is game invitational (about 16 or 17 points) with a good six card suit.

(vi)   A jump in a new suit is forcing (at least 17 points).

2NT

(i)   A rebid of the suit opened is non-forcing, with all other bids being at least invitational (you pass 2NT with a weak opener and poor suit).

(ii)   A raise to game is to play – responder must pass.

And, finally, to conclude our constructive bidding, a look at how responder continues, the fourth bid of the auction.

Continuation by Responder

(a)   When opener has made a 'limit' bid, i.e. a *non-forcing* continuation:

(i)   Any non-jump bid is not forcing and not invitational, for example: 1◇–1♡–1♠–2◇.

(ii)   Any jump rebid, or jump in opener's first suit or raise of his second suit is invitational to game (about ten to twelve points). Examples of each would be:
1◇–1♡–1♠–3♡ (shows six hearts and about 11 points);
1◇–1♠–2♣–3◇ (shows diamond support) or
1♡–1♠–2♣–3♣ (shows four card club support).

(iii)   A 'responders reverse', or a new suit at the three-level is game forcing, for example 1◇–1♡–2◇–2♠ or 1♡–1♠–2♡–3◇.

(iv)   A jump in a new suit is game forcing, for example:
1♣–1♡–2♣–3◇.

(v)   2NT is invitational, regardless of the sequence.

(b)   When opener is unlimited, i.e. has made a forcing bid, responder continues to describe his hand, with jump bids showing more than minimum values.

Quiz

Just to confirm that you have absorbed the above, answer the following questions for the sequences given below:

(a)   What is the range of openers' rebid?
(b)   Which bids in the sequence are forcing.
(c)   At what stage, if at all, is the sequence 'forcing to game'?

Sequence one. *Dealer North.*

West	North	East	South
–	1◊	Pass	1♠
Pass	3♣	Pass	3◊

Sequence two. *Dealer North.*

West	North	East	South
–	1◊	Pass	2♣
Pass	2NT	Pass	3◊

Sequence three. *Dealer North.*

West	North	East	South
–	1♠	Pass	1NT
Pass	2NT	Pass	3♣

Sequence four. *Dealer North.*

West	North	East	South
–	Pass	Pass	1◊
Pass	1♠	Pass	2♡
Pass	2♠		

Sequence five. *Dealer North.*

West	North	East	South
–	2♠	Pass	2NT
Pass	3♣	Pass	3♠

Sequence six. *Dealer North.*

West	North	East	South
–	1◊	Pass	1♡
Pass	2♡	Pass	2NT

Answers

1. (a)   18 or more points.
    (b)   All but the opening bid.
    (c)   After North's 3♣.

2. (a)   15 or 16 points.
    (b)   Both of South's.
    (c)   After South's 3◇ (with a minimum hand he must pass 2NT).

3. (a)   17 or 18 points.
    (b)   None of them.
    (c)   Never. South's 3♣ is to play, suggesting about six points and a long club suit, i.e. not enough to bid 2♣ over 1♠.

4. (a)   16-18 points.
    (b)   None of them. Because North passed as opener, his 1♠ response is no longer forcing (as he cannot have more than 11 points).
    (c)   Never.

5. (a)   Unlimited to date.
    (b)   All, except South's 3♠ bid.
    (c)   Never. Although, 3♣ is forcing, it is only forcing to 3♠ and not to game.

6. (a)   12 to 15 points.
    (b)   South's 1♡ response.
    (c)   Never.

That concludes my summary of the basic 'natural bidding system'. Like all skeletons, it requires some flesh to be put on it and that flesh will be supplied in two ways:

1. Extensive playing which will enable you to see different situations arise.
2. The additions of a *few* well chosen conventions.

Chapter 6 looks at some gadgets that should make your life easier.

6
CONVENTIONS

Imagine a round of golf without a sand wedge. To me, that would be a terrifying prospect for although it is not an essential piece of equipment to a golfer (after all, a good round will never visit a bunker), it is nonetheless very gratifying to have insurance.

Conventions are similar to that. They are not essential to playing a good bridge game, but they do help you out of a few tight spots.

Over the years, many conventions have come along and an almost equal number have sunk without trace. Those few that have stood the test of time can logically be said to be of universal benefit. I intend to concentrate on a selection from that (short) list.

If you sat down in the rubber bridge clubs of London playing a 'high-stake' game (up to £200 for each one hundred points at the top end), your partner would blurt out a phrase similar to the following:

> *'Weak, Stayman, Blackwood and Double.'*

Would you have a clue what he meant?

In English, his phrase would amount to the following:

'Weak'   – We will play a 'weak' 1NT opening (12-14 points).
'Stayman'   – A convention (see shortly).
'Blackwood' – The convention asking for Aces (see earlier).
'Double'   – The widely-accepted defence to an opening pre-empt, where a double is for takeout (see *Improve Your Bridge at Home*).

Thus armed, battle would commence for what could be vast sums of money.

The point of this tale is that top class players do not feel a need to attach a plethora of gadgets to their approach to bidding. They believe that good judgement allied to a selection of useful conventions will more than compensate for the 'Star Wars' technology of many of today's scientists.

They allow two visitors through the door, Stayman and Blackwood. We have seen Blackwood earlier (Chapter Four), now it is time for Stayman to receive its call.

The Stayman Convention

Stayman is a simple device which gains more than it loses, because of three factors:

1. It comes up frequently.
2. It is easy to use.
3. It overcomes a difficult problem.

To see the value of having some kind of conventional machinery, look at these three hands:

(a)	♠ KQ98	(b)	♠ 764	(c)	♠ K10842
	♡ 73		♡ AKJ9		♡ Q9753
	◊ KQ104		◊ 73		◊ 73
	♣ A73		♣ AJ107		♣ 7

Your partner opens 1NT (12-14) how do you respond? On (a) and (b) you could simply jump to 3NT, but what if partner had this hand opposite (a):

♠ AJ74		♠ KQ98
♡ J42	N	♡ 73
◊ A73	W E	◊ KQ104
♣ K84	S	♣ A73

or, alternatively, this hand opposite (b):

♠ AJ102		♠ 764
♡ Q1082	N	♡ AKJ9
◊ J2	W E	◊ 73
♣ KQ4	S	♣ AJ107

In both cases, 3NT would be a poor contract because it had an entire suit unprotected (hearts in (a) and diamonds in (b)). On the other hand, because the opener has four cards in responder's major, 4♠ is an excellent contract on (a) and 4♡ in (b).

But how can you find out when partner has your major? The answer, as no doubt you have guessed, is 'Stayman'. The convention simply says that:

'A 2♣ response to a 1NT opening bid asks partner if he has a four card major.'

The replies to 2♣ are:

2◇   Sorry, I do not hold either major.
2♡   I have hearts, and *maybe* spades as well.
2♠   I have spades, but definitely not hearts.

Hence, in place of our rather bow and arrow approach on hands (a) and (b), we now proceed as follows:

(a)

♠ AJ73
♡ 842
◇ A73
♣ KQ4

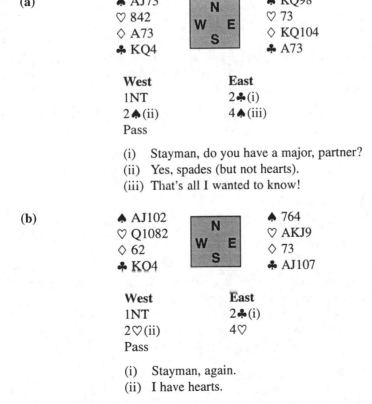

♠ KQ98
♡ 73
◇ KQ104
♣ A73

West	East
1NT	2♣(i)
2♠(ii)	4♠(iii)
Pass	

(i)   Stayman, do you have a major, partner?
(ii)   Yes, spades (but not hearts).
(iii)   That's all I wanted to know!

(b)

♠ AJ102
♡ Q1082
◇ 62
♣ KQ4

♠ 764
♡ AKJ9
◇ 73
♣ AJ107

West	East
1NT	2♣(i)
2♡(ii)	4♡
Pass	

(i)   Stayman, again.
(ii)   I have hearts.

Note in (b) that West has both hearts and spades. You may well ask 'how could we find a fit in spades'?

With a little juggling of a few cards, let us put hand (a) in here:

♠ AJ102	**N**	♠ KQ98
♡ Q1082	**W E**	♡ 73
◊ 62	**S**	◊ KQ104
♣ KQ4		♣ A73

West	East
1NT	2♣(i)
2♡(ii)	3NT(iii)
4♠(iv)	Pass

(i)   Stayman.
(ii) I have hearts ....
(iii) I don't.
(iv) ... and spades.

How can West know that it is safe to bid 4♠? The answer lies in the fact that when East uses 2♣, his partner can assume that *he must at least have one major* – otherwise why would he be interested in whether West has one?

Therefore, it is important for West (the 1NT opener) to rectify the contract to 4♠ when he holds both major suits.

I haven't commented on hand (c) as yet, and now is the time to do so, via the following question.

How would you respond to 1NT:

(a)   Without Stayman?
(b)   With Stayman?

The first part is easy, you would bid 2♠ or 2♡, depending on your intuition, and hope that your choice coincided with partner's better major. What usually happens, however, is West holds:

(a)

♠ 73	**N**	♠ K10842
♡ AJ108	**W E**	♡ Q9753
◊ AQ42	**S**	◊ 73
♣ K108		♣ 7

if you choose 2♠.

or **(b)**   ♠ AJ97      ♠ K10842
                         ♡ 84   ♡ Q9753
                         ◇ AQ42   ◇ 73
                         ♣ K108   ♣ 7

when you bid 2♡. Without Stayman we can see that you have to guess
which major to play in.

With Stayman one can bid 2♣, and then pass either 2♡ or 2♠ (2♡ in (a)
above and 2♠ in (b)). Remember, bidding Stayman does not in itself
promise strength, you could easily have a *weak hand with both majors*.

How do we cope if the reply to 2♣ is 2◇? The answer is that responder
(the Stayman bidder) continues with 2♡, which is a weak bid, asking
partner to choose between 2♡ and 2♠. He selects his longer major (or
stronger if equal), for example:

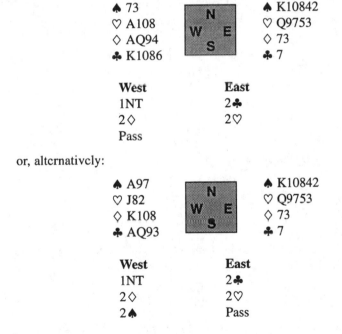

                         ♠ 73   ♠ K10842
                         ♡ A108   ♡ Q9753
                         ◇ AQ94   ◇ 73
                         ♣ K1086   ♣ 7

	West	East
	1NT	2♣
	2◇	2♡
	Pass	

or, alternatively:

                         ♠ A97   ♠ K10842
                         ♡ J82   ♡ Q9753
                         ◇ K108   ◇ 73
                         ♣ AQ93   ♣ 7

	West	East
	1NT	2♣
	2◇	2♡
	2♠	Pass

Just before we leave Stayman, here is a short quiz:

Quiz

How would you bid the following pairs of hands (West is dealer, playing a weak no trump opener)?

1.

	♠ AJ9		♠ Q1084
	♡ AJ97	N	♡ Q2
	◇ 732	W E	◇ AQJ7
	♣ Q108	S	♣ 743

2.

	♠ Q1084		♠ K653
	♡ Q1084	N	♡ J7
	◇ AKJ	W E	◇ Q82
	♣ J7	S	♣ K1093

3.

	♠ 73		♠ QJ984
	♡ AQ9	N	♡ 106532
	◇ AQ104	W E	◇ K6
	♣ Q843	S	♣ 9

Answers

1.

West	East
1NT	2♣
2♡	2NT
Pass	

East shows a raise to 2NT (inviting West to bid game with a maximum hand) *and* a four card spade suit. If West's hand was:

♠ AJ97
♡ AJ97
◇ 73
♣ Q108

he could bid 3♠ over 2NT declining the invitation to game, but preferring to play in spades (the known 4-4 fit), rather than no trumps.

2.

West	East
1NT	Pass

With only 9 points and a balanced hand, East must pass his partner's 1NT opening. If he tries Stayman and fails to find a major suit fit, he would propel the partnership to (at least) 2NT. It is a weakness of the 1NT opening that you will occasionally miss such a fit.

3.

West	East
1NT	2♣
2♢	2♡
Pass	

With two five card majors, East can use Stayman, even with a very weak hand. West must pass 2♡ or correct to 2♠, but cannot go higher.

Incidentally, you can use *Stayman over a 2NT opener* in exactly the same way.

Finally, you do not use Stayman with one five card major, for example:

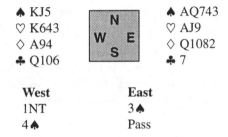

♠ KJ5		♠ AQ743
♡ K643		♡ AJ9
◇ A94		◇ Q1082
♣ Q106		♣ 7

West	East
1NT	3♠
4♠	Pass

Bidding 2♣ over 1NT would not help East determine whether his partner had three card spade support, or nothing in the suit, for example:

♠ 52
♡ K643
◇ A94
♣ KQ106

In this situation, East must tell his partner about *his* spades, rather than *ask* about opener's.

Fourth Suit Forcing (FSF)

Let me start with a bidding problem:

Game All. Dealer East.

West	North	East	South
–	–	1♡	Pass
1♠	Pass	2♣	Pass
?			

West holds:

♠ KJ986
♡ A4
◇ 753
♣ AQ4

What should he bid? Starting off in a rather negative way, what shouldn't he bid? Let us consider the options:

2♡ ⎫
2♠ ⎭ – These are weak bids and West is far too strong.

2NT ⎫
3♣ ⎪
3♡ ⎬ – All these bids are invitational to game, and again West
3♠ ⎭   (with13 points) is too strong just to invite game.

We are left with choosing a game contract ourselves, but which one should it be? 3NT, 4♡ or 4♠? I will assume you pick one, and then place an East hand consistent with the bidding, opposite your choice to show how wrong you can be!

First, those who fancy 3NT:

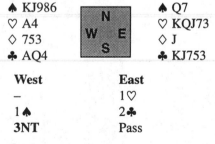

♠ KJ986   ♠ Q7
♡ A4   ♡ KQJ73
◇ 753   ◇ J
♣ AQ4   ♣ KJ753

West	East
–	1♡
1♠	2♣
3NT	Pass

Ouch!! No diamond stop.

Second, for the 4♡ bidders:

♠ KJ986   ♠ Q
♡ A4   ♡ Q9732
◇ 753   ◇ AQ10
♣ AQ4   ♣ KJ75

West	East
–	1♡
1♠	2♣
4♡	Pass

Now we are in 4♡ when 3NT is much better, you can't win! And, to save time and space, use the above example for those who bid 4♠ as well, for example:

West	East
–	1♡
1♠	2♣
4♠	Pass

So is our problem completely insoluble? It would be unless we can find out more about partner's hand *before* making a decision. The way to achieve this is via *Fourth Suit Forcing* (FSF), which operates as follows:

When the sequence is three bids old, and each one has mentioned a new *suit,* a bid of the missing or 'fourth' suit is forcing, and asks opener to make another descriptive bid. Responder can then select the final contract with more confidence and less inspired (or uninspired) guesswork.

In our example, West bids 2◊ over 2♣. He does not announce that he has diamonds as a suit (in that case he would probably bid 2NT or 3NT) but rather that he has a good hand, without a clear view of the likely final contract.

Thus armed with our new toy (FSF), how do we bid our problem hands? First, when we guessed to bid 3NT:

```
♠ KJ986          ♠ Q7
♡ A4             ♡ KQ973
◊ 753            ◊ J
♣ AJ4            ♣ KQ753
```

West	East
–	1♡
1♠	2♣
2◊ (i)	3♣ (ii)
5♣ (iii)	Pass

(i)   Fourth Suit Forcing, East *must* bid again. West wishes to know more.

(ii) Bidding clubs again shows an extra card in the suit.

(iii) Happy to have found an eight-card fit, West terminates proceedings. East/West have avoided the pitfalls of playing 3NT, 4♡ or 4♠.

And when we selected 4♡/4♠:

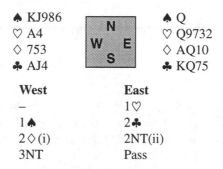

♠ KJ986		♠ Q
♡ A4		♡ Q9732
◊ 753		◊ AQ10
♣ AJ4		♣ KQ75

West	East
–	1♡
1♠	2♣
2◊(i)	2NT(ii)
3NT	Pass

(i) Fourth Suit Forcing.

(ii) With diamonds well protected, East continues with the obvious call.

Just to increase your familiarity with this, most helpful, 'waiting' bid, here are three hands to exercise on (West is dealer in all cases):

Exercise 1

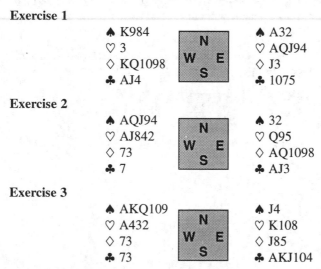

♠ K984		♠ A32
♡ 3		♡ AQJ94
◊ KQ1098		◊ J3
♣ AJ4		♣ 1075

Exercise 2

♠ AQJ94		♠ 32
♡ AJ842		♡ Q95
◊ 73		◊ AQ1098
♣ 7		♣ AJ3

Exercise 3

♠ AKQ109		♠ J4
♡ A432		♡ K108
◊ 73		◊ J85
♣ 73		♣ AKJ104

I would bid as follows:

1.

West	East
1◇	1♡
1♠	2♣(i)
2NT	3NT
Pass	

2.

West	East
1♠	2◇
2♡	3♣(i)
3♡	4♡
Pass	

3.

West	East
1♠	2♣
2♡	3◇(i)
3♠	4♠
Pass	

(i)   Fourth Suit Forcing

In example (3), West has no ideal bid over 3◇. He has shown five spades and four hearts and does not have three card support for partner. It is time to improvise.

The practical view is to treat the excellent spades as being worth 'six cards', as the suit will play satisfactorily with as little support as just ♠J. After all, East wanted further information about West's hand – that was the idea behind FSF – and the most important feature left unsaid is the *quality* of the spade suit.

As we can see, the 3♠ bid leads to an easy conclusion to the bidding and a sensible contract. That can never be bad!

I do not propose to add any other conventions to our list, instead I will briefly repeat those found earlier in the text. They are *Blackwood* and *cuebidding* for slam purposes, and the *Unassuming Cuebid* in response to partner's overcall.

If you feel deprived and wish to see more conventions, I can tell the Tournament and Club scene is for you!

Seriously, the material contained in this series is more than sufficient to play a highly competent game of bridge. Good judgement and sound card play will always overcome the convention hungry player, but I do advise that you take up those I have recommended. I feel it is the right balance between science and nature!

So to conclude, we have the following menu of conventions to add to our 'Natural' bridge system:

1. Stayman 2♣ and 3♣ (over 2NT)
Asks for four card majors over 1NT (and 2NT openings).

Bid 2♣ and partner replies with:

   2◇ No major
   2♡ Hearts (maybe spades too)
   2♠ Spades

2. Blackwood 4NT
A bid of 4NT asks about number of aces held by partner. Partner replies:

   5♣ with None (or all four Aces)
   5◇ with one ace
   5♡ with two aces
   5♠ with three aces

Then 5NT asks about Kings, with similar responses at the six level.

3. Cuebids
Tells partner about your controls (aces and voids) outside the agreed trump suit and invites him to co-operate (by bidding suits in which he has the ace).

4. Fourth Suit Forcing (FSF)
A way of telling partner you have a good hand without anything sensible to bid. Usually forces the partnership to game.

5. Unassuming Cuebids (UCBs)
Shows at least 11 points (usually balanced) with reasonable support (probably three cards) for partners *overcall*.

You will be delighted to know that your system is thus *complete!* We can move on from what is generally regarded as the hard work of playing bridge (devising and *learning* our 'system'), to the more exciting aspects of declarer play and defence.

7
ADVANCED TECHNIQUES

My wife, who is not an ardent player, suddenly took a little more interest in the book when she saw that Chapter Seven would be on 'Advanced Techniques'. Sadly, I had to assure her that it was still bridge!

Nevertheless, to me, the contents of this chapter are among the most exciting of the entire series. I suppose it is the artistic core of the game inside a basically scientific shell. Many authors let their imagination run wild at this stage, concentrating on exotic plays which rarely, if ever, are made at the table. What I propose to do, is to show you a few out-of-the-ordinary situations, but not so extreme that their rarity makes them almost valueless.

Loser on Loser

This play, which is confined to trump contracts, involves a conscious decision to fail to ruff a loser. Instead you discard a loser from another suit. This technique can be used to handle contracts where the trump suit is a little shorter than ideal. Here is an example:

North/South Game. Dealer South.

♠ K104
♡ 432
◇ 10865
♣ AQ6

♠ AQJ9
♡ 7
◇ A43
♣ KJ1095

West	North	East	South
–	–	–	1♣
Pass	1◊	Pass	1♠
Pass	2♣	Pass	2◊
Pass	3♠	Pass	4♠
All Pass			

A difficult hand to bid, hence the longer than usual sequence, leads to a delicate contract of 4♠. West begins with ♡K and continues the suit at trick two. If declarer ruffs this trick, he will be down to only three trumps and should either opponent have four spades, he will have a cooked goose!

Our 'loser on loser' play comes to the rescue. Rather than ruff, South discards a loser from another suit (in this case, diamonds). That trick had to be lost at some stage, and it doesn't really matter when from declarer's viewpoint.

The defence stubbornly continue hearts and declarer must discard again or risk the trump division being 4-2. What is all this achieving? If the defenders play hearts again, the *hand with the shorter trumps* (dummy) can ruff, thus preserving South's four card holding. Now *four* rounds of trumps can be drawn instead of three. The full hand:

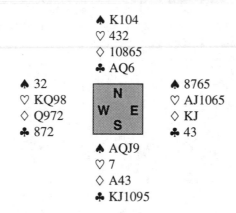

```
                    ♠ K104
                    ♡ 432
                    ◊ 10865
                    ♣ AQ6
        ♠ 32                        ♠ 8765
        ♡ KQ98         N            ♡ AJ1065
        ◊ Q972      W     E         ◊ KJ
        ♣ 872          S            ♣ 43
                    ♠ AQJ9
                    ♡ 7
                    ◊ A43
                    ♣ KJ1095
```

They only way to make 4♠ is to discard *twice* on the play of hearts, leaving declarer in control.

The loser-on-loser play can be combined with other techniques and I will cover two of these. First the '*ruffing finesse*':

Love All. Dealer South.

♠ 753
♡ QJ10
◊ 10865
♣ AQ7

♠ AK4
♡ –
◊ A4
♣ KJ1098532

West	North	East	South
–	–	–	2♣
Pass	2NT	Pass	3♣
Pass	4♣	Pass	6♣
All Pass			

South overreaches to a slam and West leads ◊ K. Is there any hope for the contract ? With an apparently certain diamond and spade loser, prospects look bleak indeed, but there is a way. Look at the full deal:

♠ 753
♡ QJ10
◊ 10865
♣ AQ7

♠ J96   ♠ Q1082
♡ A432   ♡ K98765
◊ KQ72   ◊ J93
♣ 64   ♣ –

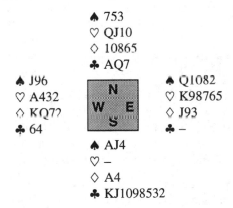

♠ AJ4
♡ –
◊ A4
♣ KJ1098532

Win ◊ A and play a club to dummy's seven. Next follow with ♡ Q and discard your losing diamond if East fails to cover. West wins the heart and plays a second diamond which you ruff. Now cross to ♣ Q to play ♡ J and pitch a spade if East plays low. On the first heart you made a 'loser on loser' play, on the second you took a ruffing finesse. All you need to succeed is for East to hold at least one heart honour.

Secondly, we can use our loser-on-loser with an '*avoidance*' play, as follows:

East/West Game. Dealer West.

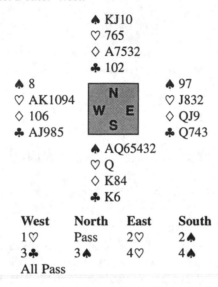

```
                    ♠ KJ10
                    ♡ 765
                    ◇ A7532
                    ♣ 102
    ♠ 8                         ♠ 97
    ♡ AK1094      N             ♡ J832
    ◇ 106       W   E           ◇ QJ9
    ♣ AJ985       S             ♣ Q743
                    ♠ AQ65432
                    ♡ Q
                    ◇ K84
                    ♣ K6
```

West	North	East	South
1♡	Pass	2♡	2♠
3♣	3♠	4♡	4♠
All Pass			

A lively sequence catapults South into 4♠ and West leads ♡A and continues with the king. The key to the hand is to be able to establish dummy's diamonds to throw South's losing clubs on. The problem on the horizon is that if East has an entry in diamonds, he will immediately play a club through the king and South will lose one heart, one diamond and two clubs.

Hence South must avoid East getting the lead at all costs, and turns to our now familiar loser on loser strategy. Let us follow how the process works. At trick two, instead of ruffing ♡K, South pitches ◇4, and then ruffs the heart continuation. Trumps are drawn, and declarer cashes ◇K, ◇A and ruffs a diamond, setting up two winners in dummy.

He returns to ♠K in dummy and takes those winners throwing both the losing clubs. Diamonds were established without ever conceding the lead to East. For the eagle-eyed amongst you, did you notice West's error?

At trick two, he must continue with ♡9 to East's jack, then the loser-on-loser play will not work. With East on lead, he can play the dreaded club through declarer's ♣K.

Before I move on, here is a hand to try for yourself (the suggested line will come at the end of the chapter – no peeping!!).

Love All. Dealer West.

♠ 532
♡ J5432
◇ 65
♣ AK4

♠ AKQJ107
♡ A
◇ 743
♣ 982

West	North	East	South
1◇	Pass	1♡	1♠
2◇	2♠	Pass	4♠
All Pass			

West leads ◇A, on which East follows with the ◇9 and continues with ◇K, East playing ◇2 (showing a doubleton). At trick three, West leads ◇Q. How do you plan the play?

End Plays

The idea behind an 'end play' (or throw-in play), is to force your opponents to do something that is to your advantage. This is usually to open up a suit which you do not wish to tackle yourself. The following example is typical of this technique:

♠ KJ94
♡ 654
◇ A85
♣ KJ9

♠ AQ10865
♡ 10
◇ 942
♣ A108

Playing in 4♠, South receives the lead of ♡K from West, who continues with another heart. To make the contract, South must find out who has ♣Q. If you played the contract and guessed wrongly, would you bemoan your luck? Would it surprise you to know that I can *guarantee* that you do not lose a club trick on this hand?

Wouldn't it be better for East/West to lead clubs? Then there would be no difficulty in locating the lady! No 'luck' required. The opponents are unlikely to volunteer to shoot themselves, so South must force them to open up the suit. Ruffing the heart at trick two, he continues by drawing two rounds of trumps, finishing in North, and ruffs dummy's last heart. This apparently pointless manoeuvre is absolutely critical to an end-play as we shall see.

Declarer plays a *diamond* to the ace and another diamond, arriving at:

♠ J9
♡ –
◇ 8
♣ KJ9

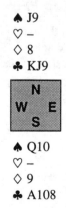

♠ Q10
♡ –
◇ 9
♣ A108

The defenders will probably take their remaining diamond trick, postponing the inevitable. They must then lead a club or concede a ruff and discard, either way South has solved his 'guess' painlessly. The full deal:

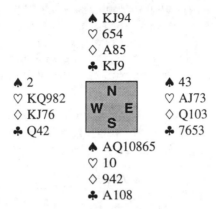

♠ KJ94
♡ 654
◇ A85
♣ KJ9

♠ 2
♡ KQ982
◇ KJ76
♣ Q42

♠ 43
♡ AJ73
◇ Q103
♣ 7653

♠ AQ10865
♡ 10
◇ 942
♣ A108

The next example shows how apparently inescapable losers can just melt away like snow. I will give all four hands this time, see if you can work out how the play should develop:

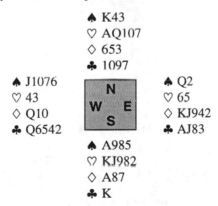

♠ K43
♡ AQ107
◇ 653
♣ 1097

♠ J1076
♡ 43
◇ Q10
♣ Q6542

♠ Q2
♡ 65
◇ KJ942
♣ AJ83

♠ A985
♡ KJ982
◇ A87
♣ K

The contract is 4♡ by South. West leads ♣4 to his partner's ace, who switches to ◇4. How can South avoid losing one spade, two diamonds and a club?

The first move is to duck the diamond switch and win the continuation of the suit, thus isolating the diamond winner in the East hand. To achieve an end-play, declarer must *eliminate* all safe exits prior to the throw-in being made. That means both dummy's clubs must be taken care of.

Hence, declarer plays a trump to dummy and ruffs a club, then back to dummy in trumps and another club ruff. With dummy's gone, stage two is complete.

Now the *coup de grâce*. With trumps drawn and clubs eliminated, it is time for the throw-in. Declarer cashes ♠A and ♠K and exits with a diamond, forcing East to win the trick. With only diamonds and clubs left, he *must* concede a ruff and discard. Declarer ruffs in hand (you nearly always ruff in the hand with fewer trumps remaining when given a ruff-and-discard), pitching the spade loser from dummy.

Almost like magic, declarer has avoided losing a spade trick. Here is one for you to try for yourself (again, the answer is at the end of the chapter).

Love All. Dealer South.

♠ A532
♡ J4
◇ KJ32
♣ J84

```
      N
  W       E
      S
```

♠ 7
♡ A10
◇ AQ10876
♣ A932

West	North	East	South
–	–	–	1◇
1♡	3◇	3♡	5◇
All Pass			

West leads ♡K; can you save the day and justify your jump to 5◇?

Dummy Reversal

Our third technique is rather quaintly called a 'dummy reversal' and is another way of getting the most out of our combined trump holding.

When we are unable to use the shorter trump suit for ruffing, we have to resort to different tactics and 'reverse dummy', i.e. ruff several times in the hand with longer trumps (usually declarer's).

Here is the technique in all its glory:

Love All. Dealer East.

♠ KJ7
♡ 10865
◇ Q76
♣ KQ4

♠ AQ1065
♡ 7
◇ 942
♣ AJ98

West	North	East	South
–	–	1NT	2♠
Pass	4♠	All Pass	

Having overbid somewhat (as usual), you arrive in 4♠. West opens the defence with ♡Q, and continues the suit (much to your relief). Although West has given you a stay of execution by failing to switch to a diamond, how can you use this to your advantage?

With four club tricks, your only chance of success appears to lie in managing six trump winners. However, there is no chance of arranging a ruff in dummy, so the task appears hopeless. Then, we hear the charge of the 5th Cavalry – a 'dummy reversal'.

We must plan to ruff three times in our hand (this added to three trumps in dummy gives us what we require). After ruffing the heart at trick two, comes a club to the queen and another heart ruff – just one more required. Over to ♣K, and our last ruff of a heart (with ♠A, just in case).

We can then draw trumps and cash our clubs for ten unlikely tricks:

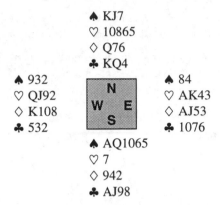

```
                    ♠ KJ7
                    ♡ 10865
                    ◇ Q76
                    ♣ KQ4
   ♠ 932                              ♠ 84
   ♡ QJ92            N                ♡ AK43
   ◇ K108       W         E           ◇ AJ53
   ♣ 532            S                 ♣ 1076
                    ♠ AQ1065
                    ♡ 7
                    ◇ 942
                    ♣ AJ98
```

Successful dummy reversals always require a great deal of 'toing and froing' between hands. Thus we must have certain pre-requisites before embarking on the journey:

1.   Dummy must possess some trump honours to expedite drawing trumps after organising the early play.
2.   Dummy must have sufficient entries to manage the necessary ruffs.

Now it's your opportunity to try a 'dummy reversal' (the answer is at the end of this chapter).

```
                    ♠ J73
                    ♡ 1098
                    ◇ A765
                    ♣KQ3

                    N
                W        E
                    S

                    ♠ 654
                    ♡ AKQJ2
                    ◇ 8
                    ♣ A542
```

South declares 4♡. The defence cash their three spade tricks before West switches to ♡4. Over to you!

The Simple Squeeze

There have been entire books written about squeezes, from the basic and very useful 'simple squeeze', to all kinds of weird and wonderful positions that I have not come across in twenty years. In my opinion, a mastery of the common layouts is more than sufficient for winning bridge.

The two most common squeezes are the 'simple' and the 'double'. First the *Simple Squeeze* which operates against *one* opponent, and is typically found where a defender has the vast majority of his side's strength. Squeezes occur more 'naturally' in no-trump contracts, because of the power of declarer's long suits, and his inability to use trumps. Here, by way of example, South plays in 3NT:

♠ 1083
♡ Q92
◇ A652
♣ KQ4

♠ KJ74
♡ KJ5
◇ J984
♣ 109

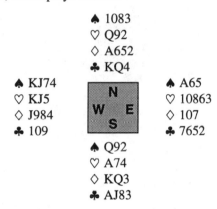

♠ A65
♡ 10863
◇ 107
♣ 7652

♠ Q92
♡ A74
◇ KQ3
♣ AJ83

West leads ♠4, and after taking the first four tricks, switches to ♣10. Correctly, declarer next cashes his long (solid) suit, clubs, exerting pressure on West. When the last club is to be played, the position is:

♠ –
♡ Q9
◇ A652
♣ –

♠ –
♡ KJ
◇ J984
♣ –

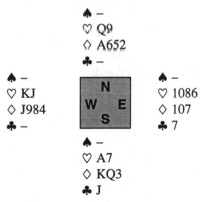

♠ –
♡ 1086
◇ 107
♣ 7

♠ –
♡ A7
◇ KQ3
♣ J

When South leads ♣J, what does West discard? If ♡J, then dummy can pitch a diamond and ♡A will bring down ♡K, while a diamond will allow the suit to be run. Can you see a flaw? How do you *know* that West has only ♡K left if he discards ♡J? Couldn't he have four hearts and three diamonds and be trying to fool you?

To avoid this problem and to be *certain* that the squeeze has worked, it is correct technique for South to cash ♡A *before* playing the last club, i.e.

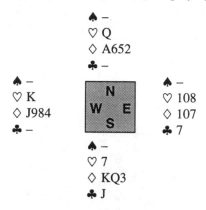

Now instead of having to guess that West has blanked his ♡K, declarer will actually see ♡K on the table! If a diamond is discarded, South can throw ♡Q from dummy, mentally thanking her for a job well done!

So a simple squeeze operates against one opponent when he has control of at least two suits. The 'threats', or 'menaces' as they are often called, do not have to be in the same hand. A squeeze would also work on this layout:

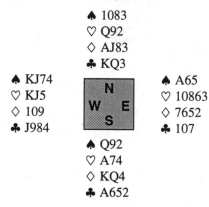

After four rounds of spades and a diamond switch, declarer cashes ♡ A and the remaining diamonds. This is the position before the last winner is to be played.

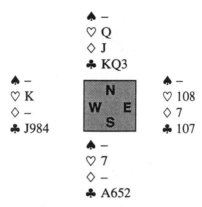

Once again West is stuck when ◊ J is cashed, even though one menace (♡ Q) is in the North hand, and the other (the long club) is in South's.

However, a squeeze will not operate if the defender sits over (i.e. discards *after*) the hand with *all* the menaces. West would be safe on this hand:

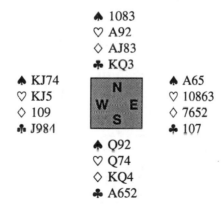

The play follows its normal course (four rounds of spades and a diamond switch), but look what happens when we arrive at the crucial point:

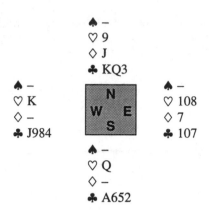

♠ –
♥ 9
♦ J
♣ KQ3

♠ –   ♠ –
♥ K   ♥ 108
♦ –   ♦ 7
♣ J984   ♣ 107

♠ –
♥ Q
♦ –
♣ A652

With West discarding after South, he simply 'follows suit'. If ♥Q is pitched, he plays ♥K and if a club is discarded, West does the same. Note that if the ♥9 and ♥10 were interchanged, the squeeze would operate. South could discard ♥Q on ♦J, and ♥10 (now in North) would become a threat to West, as East could no longer be of assistance.

Here is a 'simple squeeze' to try for yourself.

Love All. Dealer East.

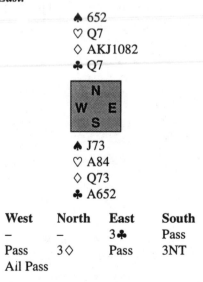

♠ 652
♥ Q7
♦ AKJ1082
♣ Q7

♠ J73
♥ A84
♦ Q73
♣ A652

West	North	East	South
–	–	3♣	Pass
Pass	3♦	Pass	3NT
All Pass			

West cashes ♠A K Q and 10, everyone following to the first three rounds. He now switches to ♥10, and you …?

The Double Squeeze

The double squeeze operates against both opponents simultaneously. It is rarer than the simple squeeze and often requires more care and attention to detail. Nevertheless, most of the same principles apply, in that you need threats or menaces, but this time against both opponents. Also, there must be a suit which they *both* guard. This is the classic set-up:

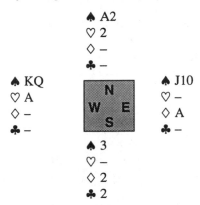

```
            ♠ A2
            ♡ 2
            ◇ −
            ♣ −
  ♠ KQ                   ♠ J10
  ♡ A      N             ♡ −
  ◇ −    W   E           ◇ A
  ♣ −      S             ♣ −
            ♠ 3
            ♡ −
            ◇ 2
            ♣ 2
```

South plays his master ♣2 (in a no trump or ♣ contract) and wins the last three tricks. To 'guard' ♡2 West must keep ♡A, so he discards a spade. The heart having done its work can now be safely pitched from dummy and it is East's turn to play. He must protect ◇2 in South's hand with his ace, and he too lets a spade go. Now both opponents have only one spade left, so South leads a spade to the ace and ♠2 wins the last trick.

From theory to the heat of battle:

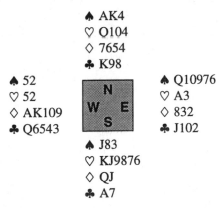

```
            ♠ AK4
            ♡ Q104
            ◇ 7654
            ♣ K98
  ♠ 52                   ♠ Q10976
  ♡ 52      N            ♡ A3
  ◇ AK109  W   E         ◇ 832
  ♣ Q6543    S           ♣ J102
            ♠ J83
            ♡ KJ9876
            ◇ QJ
            ♣ A7
```

West	North	East	South
–	1NT	Pass	4♡
All Pass			

The defence start with two rounds of diamonds, and then switch to ♠5. South wins the ace in dummy, and plays ♡Q to East's ace, who exits with his second heart. How should declarer continue?

First he has to make dummy's diamond holding into a threat against West, so win the trump return in dummy and ruff a diamond. Then cash ♠A (to 'unblock' the suit), and play out all South's trumps. This is the desired position before the *coup de grâce* is applied:

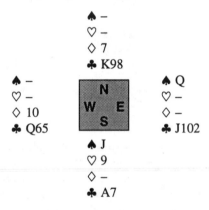

```
                    ♠ –
                    ♡ –
                    ◊ 7
                    ♣ K98
      ♠ –                        ♠ Q
      ♡ –          N             ♡ –
      ◊ 10      W     E          ◊ –
      ♣ Q65        S             ♣ J102
                    ♠ J
                    ♡ 9
                    ◊ –
                    ♣ A7
```

All the elements of a successful double squeeze are in place. When South plays ♡9, West has to pitch a club or ◊7 in North would be a winner, North then throws ◊7 and East ... he cannot discard ♠Q without letting the jack win a trick, so he too discards a club. Q.E.D.

Here is your example (take your time, squeezes are *never* easy):

Love All. Dealer West.

♠ AKJ2
♡ 10632
◊ Q98
♣ QJ

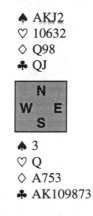

♠ 3
♡ Q
◊ A753
♣ AK109873

West	North	East	South
4♡	Pass	Pass	5♣
Pass	6♣	All Pass	

West leads ♡A and ♡K, East discarding ◊2 on the second round. Over to you. (Once again the answer is given at the end of the chapter.)

Safety Plays and Suit Combinations

A 'safety play', as suggested by its name, is a technique to use when it is paramount to avoid disaster. In bridge terms that translates to when your contract appears completely assured, and you can afford the luxury of catering for things to go badly. It is an insurance policy, and works in much the same way.

The essence of a safety play is to ensure that you lose *no more* than a specified number of tricks in a suit. Your 'premium' is the fact that you often concede an unnecessary trick when making such a play. Consider this example:

♠ K974
♡ 73
◇ KQ42
♣ Q82

♠ AJ65
♡ 65
◇ J103
♣ AK73

As South, you are playing in 4♠. The defence cash two rounds of hearts and switch to a club. With a diamond still to lose, you need to negotiate spades without loss. Therefore, you win the club, cash ♠K and play a spade, finessing ♠J when East follows low.

Your method of handling spades was pre-determined by the fact that you could not afford to lose a trick in the suit. Would that change if there was 'slack' in the contract? Now we have the same hand, but with a little more strength:

♠ K974
♡ 73
◇ KQ42
♣ Q82

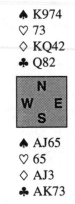

♠ AJ65
♡ 65
◇ AJ3
♣ AK73

Again, you are South in a contract of 4♠ and the defence begin with two rounds of hearts, followed by a club switch. Your contract is very good and will be made as long as you only lose (at most) one trick in trumps.

Accordingly, you win the club, play ♠K and another spade but East shows out. You are going to be defeated now. Here is the full deal:

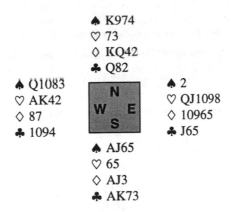

```
              ♠ K974
              ♡ 73
              ◇ KQ42
              ♣ Q82
♠ Q1083      ┌──────────┐      ♠ 2
♡ AK42       │    N     │      ♡ QJ1098
◇ 87         │  W   E   │      ◇ 10965
♣ 1094       │    S     │      ♣ J65
             └──────────┘
              ♠ AJ65
              ♡ 65
              ◇ AJ3
              ♣ AK73
```

Unlucky? Partly yes, but mainly no! With the aid of a 'safety' play, you could have assured your contract against *any* 4-1 division of spades. This is how.

Let us consider the spade suit in isolation:

♠ K974

♠ AJ65

The objective is to lose at most one trick, and we are happy to pay an insurance premium of having exactly one loser, even if it could have been avoided by 'normal' play. Just as long as we can guarantee that we will not have a second loser.

We must guard against both these situations *simultaneously:*

(a)   ♠ K974

          ♠ Q1083   ♠ 2

                           ♠ AJ65

(b)   ♠ K974

          ♠ 2   ♠ Q1083

                           ♠ AJ65

Take a moment to reflect on how you could do that before reading on.

We achieve our 'safe' play by bringing ♠9 into the play. First we cash ♠A and then continue with a low spade. If West follows suit with a low card we insert the nine, covering ourselves against position (a). If West shows out, we rise with ♠K and continue with a third round towards the jack. Again, we lose exactly one trick.

Safety plays do not have much appeal, however, because few of us like paying insurance. You frequently lose an unnecessary trick , for example, let me replace the spade suits above with a couple of more common layouts:

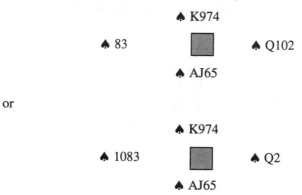

or

The safety play of leading ♠A and following with a spade to the nine will lose a trick on both of these occasions, when the normal percentage play would not. Hence their use tends to be confined to contracts where you expect to make *at least one overtrick*. Such contracts are, unfortunately, quite rare *and* to have a suit where a safety play is available as well, is even rarer.

However, to know the optimum way of tackling suits is crucial to our development of declarer play, and hence I have a rather lengthier quiz than usual. Parts I and II concentrate on how to play particular suit combinations, and then there is the normal play problem with the answer at the end of the chapter.

Quiz

1. How do you play the following suits to *maximise* your tricks?

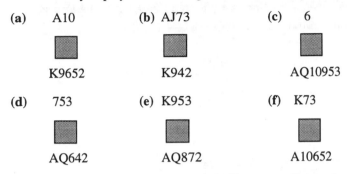

(a) A10	**(b)** AJ73	**(c)** 6
K9652	K942	AQ10953
(d) 753	**(e)** K953	**(f)** K73
AQ642	AQ872	A10652

2. How do you play the following suits if you can afford to lose one trick *at most*?

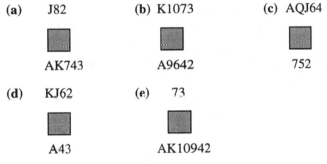

(a) J82	**(b)** K1073	**(c)** AQJ64
AK743	A9642	752
(d) KJ62	**(e)** 73	
A43	AK10942	

3. How do you play the following hands in 3NT on the lead of ♡J.

♠ J84
♡ AK
◇ 8432
♣ A943

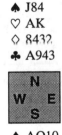

♠ AQ10
♡ 64
◇ A765
♣ KJ52

Answers

1. **(a)** We can make four tricks routinely whenever the suit divides 3-3, and we can improve on this by careful use of the intermediate cards. Consider the following circumstances:

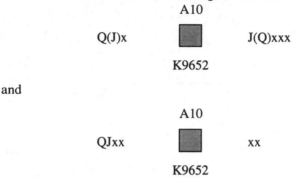

A10

Q(J)x   J(Q)xxx

K9652

and

A10

QJxx   xx

K9652

by leading *low from South and inserting the ten* from North, we will win the all-important fourth trick on all the above layouts.

(b) Our classic 'safety play' suit from earlier, but to make the maximum number of tricks, we revert to the finesse. However, we can improve on the 'natural' play of cashing the king, by catering for this layout:

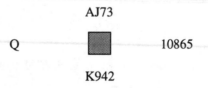

AJ73

Q   10865

K942

If we begin with a *low card from South* and capture West's queen, we will then be able to finesse through East's ten.

(c) If East and West have three cards each and one has the jack, whilst the other has the king, we just have to guess well. But if West has two cards including an honour, *we should finesse the queen*:

(i)   6

Jx   Kxxx

AQ10953

(ii)

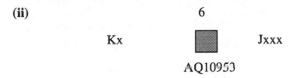

6

Kx   Jxxx

AQ10953

In (a), the finesse of the queen, followed by cashing the ace will give us five tricks, because West's jack is nullified. In (b), even if we guess correctly and insert the ten on the first round, we still have to concede a later trick to the jack after cashing the AQ. Our good guess has gained us nothing!

(d) *Cash the ace first*, before crossing to North and leading low to the queen. The defenders must win at least one trick anyway, so it does not matter which one. Our play gains in one position:

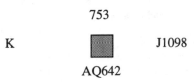

753

K   J1098

AQ642

Not very likely I hear you say, but over a year (let alone a lifetime) of bridge these minute chances add up. This extra care and attention is akin to consistently playing a round of golf one shot better.

(e) We can guard against one of the 4-0 breaks, but only when East has four.

K953

Void   J1064

AQ872

First, *cash the king* (start from the hand with one top honour), then you can collect East's holding by virtue of *two finesses*. Note, how adding the ten changes the play:

K953

AQ1082

Now we must cash the ace (i.e. the hand with two honours), because we can pick up J764 in *either* hand.

(f) *Cash the king* and continue from North. If East follows a second time, insert the ten:

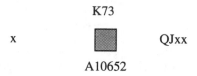

K73

x   QJxx

A10652

You will save one trick if East has QJxx in the suit, otherwise it makes no difference.

The list of examples is by no means exhaustive, but does give you a flavour of the techniques involved. The key is to imagine a bad 'break' in a suit, and see if you can cope with it, *whilst not diminishing your trick taking potential when all goes smoothly.*

Such an approach is different to our next group of problems. Now we will be consciously following a theoretically 'poor' line of play, in an attempt to limit our losses. In other words, true 'safety plays'.

2. (a) *Cash the ace and then lead low towards the jack.* You restrict your losers to one in the following situations:

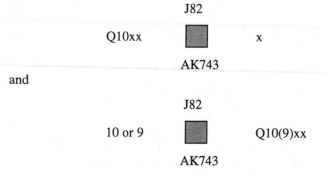

J82

Q10xx   x

AK743

and

J82

10 or 9   Q10(9)xx

AK743

(b) *Lead low from either hand and insert the ten (or nine)* if the next hand follows, guarding against QJ85 in one hand:

K1073

QJ85   Void

A9642

if you accidentally led the king first, you would lose two tricks.

(c)   *Lead low to the ace* to cater for:

AQJ64

10983      K

752

Next, return to the South hand and play up to the QJ (West may have Kxxx, so you cannot necessarily afford to lead the queen from North).

(d)   *Play low to the king, low to the ace and then lead up to the jack.* If the suit divides 3-3, you cannot lose more than one trick. The play also succeeds whenever West has four cards, particularly this layout where you cannot afford to finesse the jack:

KJ62

xxxx   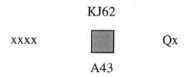   Qx

A43

(e)   *Cash the ace, then cross to North and lead low to the ten*, in case East has QJxx.

That concludes the section on Advanced Techniques, and I hope you are excited by what you have seen. Please do not think that you can 'never master' what is contained here because, as with every new idea, practice makes perfect. Always be aware of these plays, but be careful not to get carried away 'looking for the spectacular', and forget the bread and butter approach. 95% of hands can be played quite effectively without reference to anything 'clever'.

Finally, take one thought with you. *If a contract appears safe, guard against the unexpected whenever possible.* These situations can often be spotted because you expect to make at least one overtrick when suits divide 'normally'.

Finally, I must return to the various play problems I gave you earlier, or had you forgotten?

Answers to Play Problems

1.   Loser on Loser

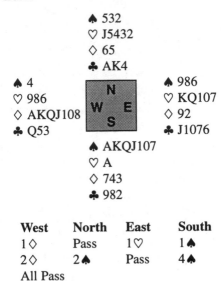

```
               ♠ 532
               ♡ J5432
               ◇ 65
               ♣ AK4
  ♠ 4                      ♠ 986
  ♡ 986            N       ♡ KQ107
  ◇ AKQJ108    W     E     ◇ 92
  ♣ Q53            S       ♣ J1076
               ♠ AKQJ107
               ♡ A
               ◇ 743
               ♣ 982
```

West	North	East	South
1◇	Pass	1♡	1♠
2◇	2♠	Pass	4♠
All Pass			

West leads ◇ A and continues with the king and queen after East peters to show a doubleton.

You could try ♠5 and pray that East had been dealt precisely a singleton ♠4, and cannot overruff! A far better line is to pitch ♣4 from dummy on the third round of diamonds (loser on loser) and hope to ruff a club later. West will probably switch to a heart, you win with the ace and cash ♠AK hoping the suit divides 2-2. Next, take ♣AK ruff a heart high in hand, and then ruff your remaining club in dummy.

You succeed whenever trumps are 2-2, or if East has 4 clubs with his 3 spades (as in the layout above). In that case, he cannot discard a club on the third round of diamonds and over-ruff dummy later. This would be effective defence had East held:

```
               ♠ 986
               ♡ KQ1097
               ◇ 92
               ♣ J107
```

2.   Endplays

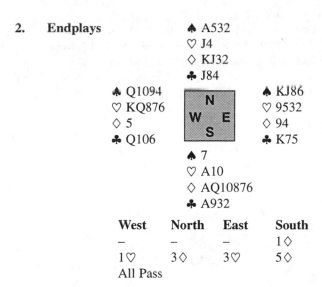

♠ A532
♡ J4
◊ KJ32
♣ J84

♠ Q1094   ♠ KJ86
♡ KQ876   ♡ 9532
◊ 5   ◊ 94
♣ Q106   ♣ K75

♠ 7
♡ A10
◊ AQ10876
♣ A932

West	North	East	South
–	–	–	1◊
1♡	3◊	3♡	5◊
All Pass			

West leads ♡K; how do you propose to make the contract? You are facing one heart and two club losers, so prospects are not great. To have any chance, you need to engineer that East/West tackle clubs, rather than you. An 'end-play' must be found to force your opponents to defend in your best interests.

With this in mind, you need to 'eliminate' spades to ensure that no safe exit exists. Win ♡A, play a spade to the ace and ruff a spade. Back to ◊J for another ruff, and finally to ◊K to remove dummy's last spade.

The scene is set. You exit expectantly with a heart which West must win. This is the position you hope for:

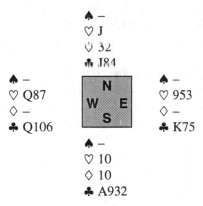

♠ –
♡ J
◊ 32
♣ J84

♠ –   ♠ –
♡ Q87   ♡ 953
◊ –   ◊ –
♣ Q106   ♣ K75

♠ –
♡ 10
◊ 10
♣ A932

In with ♡Q, West must lead a club or concede a 'ruff and discard'. If it is
♣6, you play low in dummy, win ♣K with your ace, and lead towards
dummy's jack. If it is ♣Q you duck (!) the trick, forcing West to continue
the suit. Either way, you restrict your club losers to one. A satisfying
contract to make, I am sure you will agree.

3.   Dummy Reversal

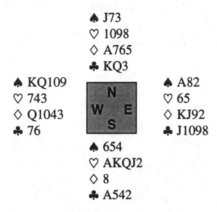

```
                        ♠ J73
                        ♡ 1098
                        ◇ A765
                        ♣ KQ3
        ♠ KQ109                        ♠ A82
        ♡ 743            N             ♡ 65
        ◇ Q1043      W     E          ◇ KJ92
        ♣ 76            S             ♣ J1098
                        ♠ 654
                        ♡ AKQJ2
                        ◇ 8
                        ♣ A542
```

The defence cash three spade tricks against your 4♡ contract and switch
to a trump. You could put all your eggs in the club basket and rely on the
suit dividing 3-3, but you can improve on those odds considerably as
follows.

Win the trump switch in hand, cross to ◇A and ruff a diamond high. Then
cross to dummy's ♡9 (by leading your carefully preserved ♡2) to ruff a
second diamond. Next play a club to the queen to take a third ruff, and
finally return to dummy with ♣K to draw the outstanding trump. By
scoring *three* ruffs in hand, you have developed an extra trick.

Note that you should cross to dummy *first* in trumps, because you will find
out (before it is too late) how the suit lies. If they do not divide evenly, you
must revert to drawing trumps, and hope that clubs split 3-3. The 'dummy
reversal' cannot cope with a 4-1 break (because you are unable to draw
trumps).

4.   The Simple Squeeze

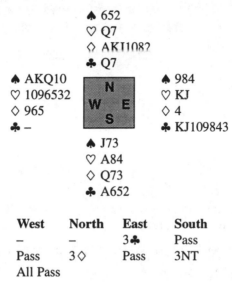

```
                ♠ 652
                ♡ Q7
                ◇ AKJ1082
                ♣ Q7
 ♠ AKQ10                      ♠ 984
 ♡ 1096532                    ♡ KJ
 ◇ 965                        ◇ 4
 ♣ −                          ♣ KJ109843
                ♠ J73
                ♡ A84
                ◇ Q73
                ♣ A652
```

West	North	East	South
–	–	3♣	Pass
Pass	3◇	Pass	3NT
All Pass			

You are playing in 3NT and West begins the defence with four rounds of spades. With eight top tricks, you are searching for the elusive ninth, but prospects are bleak. A squeeze may be required.

With East known to guard clubs, it is he who must have ♡K. Before getting embroiled in that, you must discard carefully from dummy at trick four. Should you pitch a heart or a club? A club is the answer so that you can retain ♡Q as a menace against East.

You must also be watchful when West switches to ♡10, *not* to cover with the queen. A good defender will never have switched from ♡K in this situation.

After winning ♡A, cash the diamonds to arrive at this position with three cards left:

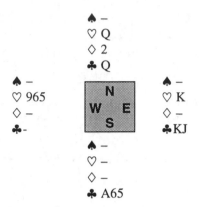

When North plays ◇2, East is squeezed between hearts and clubs. If he lets ♡K go, dummy's queen will be high, and a club discard will allow South to win the last two tricks.

Hard to believe that such a series of plays could be called a 'simple' squeeze.

2.   The Double Squeeze

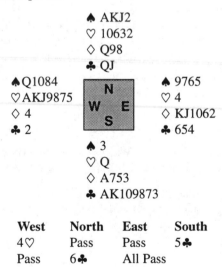

West	North	East	South
4♡	Pass	Pass	5♣
Pass	6♣	All Pass	

West leads ♡A and ♡K against your over-optimistic 6♣ contract, East discarding ◇2 on the second round. With only ten top tricks, a great deal of luck is required to land the slam. The spade finesse *must* work, *and* a squeeze needs to provide the twelfth trick.

After ruffing ♡K, draw all the trumps and lay down ◇A (in case the king falls). Then, continue with trumps leaving all dummy's spades intact. This is the hoped-for end-position when the last trump appears:

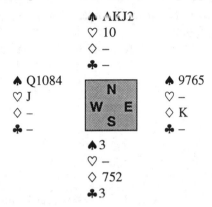

                    ♠ AKJ2
                    ♡ 10
                    ◇ –
                    ♣ –

♠ Q1084   ♠ 9765
♡ J   ♡ –
◇ –   ◇ K
♣ –   ♣ –

                    ♠ 3
                    ♡ –
                    ◇ 752
                    ♣ 3

On ♣3, West must discard a spade in order to keep ♡J, now dummy's ♡10 can be finally released, having performed a valuable service. East needs to retain ◇K, so he too lets a spade go.

Declarer finesses ♠J at trick 10 and when it holds the trick, the other spades are good, thus making a most improbable slam. Note how the 'menaces' work. Hearts against West, and diamonds against East, both forcing discards in the suit you are trying to run – spades. A classic 'double' squeeze.

5.   Safety Plays

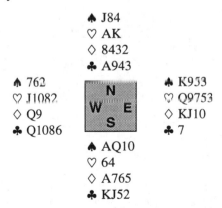

                    ♠ J84
                    ♡ AK
                    ◇ 8432
                    ♣ A943

♠ 762   ♠ K953
♡ J1082   ♡ Q9753
◇ Q9   ◇ KJ10
♣ Q1086   ♣ 7

                    ♠ AQ10
                    ♡ 64
                    ◇ A765
                    ♣ KJ52

Against South's 3NT contract, West leads ♡J, what is the best chance of making nine tricks?

With six 'top' tricks, you need to develop three more quickly. The black suits offer hope of reaching your goal in the time available, but care must be taken to combine *all* your chances.

Clubs can *safely* be played for three tricks (see earlier), or you could try for four in normal fashion. The problem is that at this stage you don't know how many tricks you need from the suit. The answer to this dilemma lies in another place.

If the spade finesse is onside, you have 3 spades, two hearts and one diamond on top and hence require only 3 club tricks – you can make the safety play of ♣K and a club to dummy's nine.

If the spade finesse loses, however, you need four club tricks and hence must play the suit in the conventional way, a low club to the jack (not the ace first, remember).

Hence, win ♡A at trick one and lead ♠J from dummy to 'discover' whether you need three club tricks or four. You must repeat the spade finesse if it wins, just to confirm the position of ♠K. If the finesse succeeds, make the safety play in clubs.

Finding out how one suit lies in order to deduce how to play another is often called a *Discovery* play. Maybe I'll come back to such plays in a later (yet to be commissioned!) book, for now it is time to move on.

8
INFERENCES
FROM THE BIDDING

Every bid has its price. It is measured in terms of providing the opposition with information about your hand. In this chapter we will learn how to turn the tables and extract the maximum advantage possible from our opponents' bidding (or lack of it). We will make them pay heavily for daring to interrupt our auction.

Let me start with a fairly simple example to show the theme:

Love All. Dealer West.

```
            ♠ 932
            ♡ 752
            ◇ K94
            ♣ KJ97
```

```
            ♠ A54
            ♡ Q93
            ◇ A62
            ♣ A1084
```

West	North	East	South
1♡	Pass	Pass	1NT(i)
All Pass			

    (i)   The protective no trump overcall (see earlier chapter).

Against your 1NT contract, West leads ♡J to East's ace, who returns the suit. Stop now. Your contract depends on who has ♣Q, but you should already know that. Why?

You could say West must have ♣Q, because he *opened* the bidding. You would be right, but for the wrong reason!

It is the negative inference that East *cannot have the ♣Q* that is germane. When East passed West's opening bid, he was showing at most 5 points. Having played ♡A already, he has effectively denied holding ♣Q as well.

How about this hand?

Love All. Dealer West.

```
              ♠ 932
              ♡ 93
              ◊ Q10864
              ♣ AQJ
           ┌──────────┐
           │    N     │
           │  W    E  │
           │    S     │
           └──────────┘
              ♠ A6
              ♡ Q64
              ◊ AKJ9753
              ♣ 6
```

West	North	East	South
Pass	Pass	Pass	1◊
1♡	3◊	Pass	5◊
All Pass			

West leads ♡A on which East plays ♡2 and switches to ♠4 to the king and your ace. The trump is drawn painlessly and the contract hinges on who has ♣K. *Faites vos jeux* before reading on.

Although West's overcall makes it theoretically more likely that he holds ♣K, this time we can work out that he does not. All the clues we require are there in front of us. We start by piecing together West's hand, and in particular his high cards, and see what we can deduce.

First, we can place West with (at least) ♡AK, from the opening lead and East's signal. Secondly, the spade switch shows that we can add ♠Q (because East would play ♠Q and not ♠K if he held ♠KQ). That leaves West with at least 9 points in the majors. Finally, *la pièce de résistance,* is that West cannot have as many as 12 points, because *he 'passed' as dealer*. Thus, he does not possess ♣K, because he would have opened 1♡.

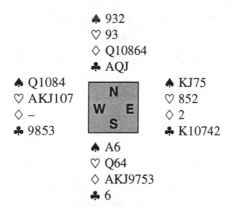

♠ 932
♡ 93
◊ Q10864
♣ AQJ

♠ Q1084   ♠ KJ75
♡ AKJ107   ♡ 852
◊ –   ◊ 2
♣ 9853   ♣ K10742

♠ A6
♡ Q64
◊ AKJ9753
♣ 6

Hence, you play a club to the ace and confidently lead ♣Q from dummy, discarding your losing spade if it is not covered (a ruffing finesse). In the end you will lose only two hearts and make your contract.

Notice how we review the evidence from two distinct areas:

1. The bidding, or lack of it.
2. The defence.

This combination is extremely powerful, as we shall see.

Sometimes our deductions can lead us to make what appear on the surface to be strange plays:

♠ Q107
♡ 10875
◊ K98
♣ KQ4

♠ KJ9865
♡ 9
◊ AJ7
♣ J108

West	North	East	South
–	–	1NT(i)	2♠
Pass	3♠	Pass	4♠
All Pass			

(i)   12-14

As South you arrive in an ambitious but by no means hopeless, contract of 4♠, after East has opened a weak no trump. West begins with ♡K and a second heart to East's ace, which you ruff.

A trump goes to East's ace, who continues with a second trump. How do you find out who has ◊Q? As soon as an opponent defines his point-count within close boundaries, as East has done with his opening bid of 1NT, you have more opportunity to determine exactly who has what.

Here, for example, we already know East has ♠A, ♡A and (because he cannot even reach 12 points without it) ♣A. That leaves both options open: he may have ◊Q or he may not. We do not seem to have moved very far forward. Is there anything else we can discover, which may throw light on the problem?

The answer is that an apparently insignificant card, ♡J, will tell us what we want. We capture the second trump in dummy and ruff a heart, then continue with a club to the queen (and East's ace), and win the club return in dummy. Now the last heart is ruffed, on which *East follows with ♡J*. At the eleventh hour, we have discovered the key piece of information. There is no longer any need to 'guess' who has ◊Q, we know.

East has 13 points already accounted for and *cannot have* ◊Q. We must play the diamond suit in a highly unusual way. First lead ◊J from hand, forcing West to cover with the queen, and then (after it is covered), lead ◊9 from dummy and hope that East has ◊10. This ploy is often called a *backwards finesse*.

The full deal:

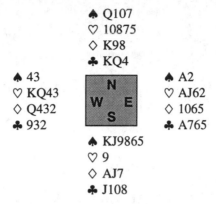

```
                    ♠ Q107
                    ♡ 10875
                    ◇ K98
                    ♣ KQ4
 ♠ 43                              ♠ A2
 ♡ KQ43              N             ♡ AJ62
 ◇ Q432         W        E         ◇ 1065
 ♣ 932               S            ♣ A765
                    ♠ KJ9865
                    ♡ 9
                    ◇ AJ7
                    ♣ J108
```

Here is another example on the same theme:

North/South Game. Dealer East.

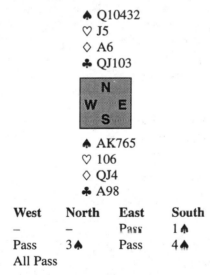

```
                    ♠ Q10432
                    ♡ J5
                    ◇ A6
                    ♣ QJ103
                     N
                W        E
                     S
                    ♠ AK765
                    ♡ 106
                    ◇ QJ4
                    ♣ A98
```

West	North	East	South
–	–	Pass	1♠
Pass	3♠	Pass	4♠
All Pass			

West leads ♡4 to East's king, who cashes ♡A before switching to ♣2. There seems no alternative but to finesse, or is there? What do you think?

Consider the bidding, or in this case, the lack of it. East passed first in hand and has shown up with ♡AK. Therefore, he cannot both ◇K and ♣K as well. If you rise with ♣A, and East proves to have ♣K all along, you will still make your contract, because *the diamond finesse is bound to succeed*. All you will lose is an overtrick.

Sometimes, playing ♣A can bring a spectacular reward, however:

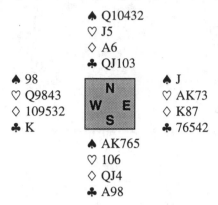

                    ♠ Q10432
                    ♡ J5
                    ♦ A6
                    ♣ QJ103
    ♠ 98   ♠ J
    ♡ Q9843   ♡ AK73
    ♦ 109532   ♦ K87
    ♣ K   ♣ 76542
                    ♠ AK765
                    ♡ 106
                    ♦ QJ4
                    ♣ A98

Credit East with good defence. He knew if he switched passively to a trump, and then won ♦K at a later stage, it would be obvious that he couldn't hold ♣K. He put you to the test before you had all the facts, and he tried a sneaky ♣2 to put you off your guard to boot. Note also how ♣A is akin to an advanced form of safety play, often giving up an extra trick (when ♣K is with East) in order to cater for a specific, but unlikely, situation.

Occasionally a defender curses his luck, because he knows something nasty is about to befall him, and there is nothing he can do about it. Take the East chair on the hand below:

Game All. Dealer North.

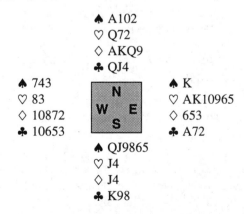

                    ♠ A102
                    ♡ Q72
                    ♦ AKQ9
                    ♣ QJ4
    ♠ 743   ♠ K
    ♡ 83   ♡ AK10965
    ♦ 10872   ♦ 653
    ♣ 10653   ♣ A72
                    ♠ QJ9865
                    ♡ J4
                    ♦ J4
                    ♣ K98

West	North	East	South
–	1◇	1♡	1♠
Pass	2NT	Pass	3♠
Pass	4♠	All Pass	

Can you see any reason to be unhappy, other than having to play with a partner who holds similar cards to me? Look at how things may develop.

Against 4♠, West leads ♡8 to East's king. He continues with ♡A, ♣A and another club. South wins in hand and immediately plays a spade to the *ace*, felling the king, just as East had dreaded all along. Why did declarer not take the trump finesse? To answer that ask yourself why East had not pressed on with hearts after cashing ♣A. Whenever *West* held ♠K, that defence would defeat the contract, by enabling him to over-ruff declarer. But if *East* held ♠K, declarer would trump the third round of hearts with ♠Q, and West could not overruff, thus marking East with the key card. East knew that would happen if he played a third round of hearts, so he stuck to clubs.

By that logic it is East who must hold ♠K, and the only chance to make the contract is to hope it is singleton.

Before we leave inferences from the bidding, here is a hand to play:

♠ J843
♡ AQ75
◇ 98
♣ K42

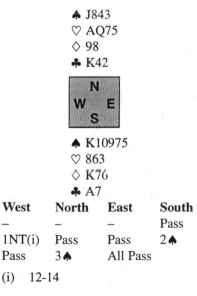

♠ K10975
♡ 863
◇ K76
♣ A7

West	North	East	South
–	–	–	Pass
1NT(i)	Pass	Pass	2♠
Pass	3♠	All Pass	

(i)   12-14

West leads ♣Q, how do you propose to play the hand?

West's point-count is well-defined, so it is incumbent upon us to try and discover as much as we can about the location of his high cards, *before* we make our key guess in trumps.

Therefore, we win ♣A and finesse ♡Q at trick two, which we are pleased to see holds the trick. Next comes a diamond to the king and West's ace. He continues with ♡K taken in dummy.

On a low spade lead East follows with ♠2, armed with what you can deduce about West's hand, do you play the king or the nine? Let us put the clues together. We can fill in the following honours with certainty because we have seen them:

♠ ?

♡ K

◇ A

♣ QJ

However, West's play of ♡K is strongly suggestive of holding ♡J to support it. That means we can account for 11 points with some degree of confidence, and therefore West cannot have ♠A as well. We rise with ♠K and exit a spade felling timber all around us:

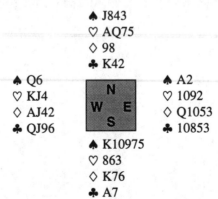

♠ J843
♡ AQ75
◇ 98
♣ K42

♠ Q6		♠ A2
♡ KJ4		♡ 1092
◇ AJ42		◇ Q1053
♣ QJ96		♣ 10853

♠ K10975
♡ 863
◇ K76
♣ A7

We lose one spade, one heart and two diamond tricks to scramble home in our slightly precarious contract.

Always consider the opponents bidding or lack of it, because it can lead to surprising conclusions about how the cards are placed.

9
ADVANCED SIGNALLING

Advanced signalling cannot be taken to mean the following, heard at a bridge club a few years ago:

After her partner led a card, declarer turned to an old lady and asked:

'Do you make fourth best leads?'
'We do,' she replied, 'but that isn't one.'
'How can you tell?' enquired declarer.
'Because it's a singleton,' continued the lady proud of her confidence in the partnership 'methods'.
'Why?', asked a somewhat bewildered declarer.
'She led it with her left hand and we always lead singletons with our left hand,' came the assured reply.

Signalling should begin with the opening lead, however, because we need to give partner an idea of our approximate holding in the suit. The only way this can be done, fairly I hasten to add, is by ascribing a meaning to the card we lead, for example:

A *low card* normally indicates length and an honour at the top of the suit.
A *high intermediate* (7, 8, or 9) may deny an honour or imply shortage.
An *honour* usually shows a sequence of which the card led is at the top.

To advance our signalling techniques, we must use 'idle cards', i.e. those which have no relevance to the play, to their best advantage. Primarily, our focus when giving signals is to direct partner's attention to a particular suit. Look at this defensive problem:

Love All. Dealer West.

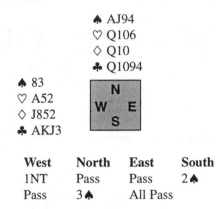

                    ♠ AJ94
                    ♡ Q106
                    ◇ Q10
                    ♣ Q1094
    ♠ 83
    ♡ A52
    ◇ J852
    ♣ AKJ3

West	North	East	South
1NT	Pass	Pass	2♠
Pass	3♠	All Pass	

As West, you lead ♣K (requesting partner gives you the count, the ♣A would ask for 'attitude') and East plays ♣8. You continue with ♣A and East shows out, discarding ♡3. It is clear that you can defeat the contract if East can obtain *two* ruffs. The first is easy, how do you ensure that partner returns a heart to get his second ruff?

The answer is that you lead a *high* card to request that partner plays *the higher ranking suit*. Conversely, a low card asks for the lower ranking. Here we play ♣J, encouraging partner to lead hearts after he ruffs (trumps are always ignored in the calculation). Just change the cards a little and ....

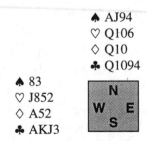

                    ♠ AJ94
                    ♡ Q106
                    ◇ Q10
                    ♣ Q1094
    ♠ 83
    ♡ J852
    ◇ A52
    ♣ AKJ3

Now we play ♣3 at trick three to indicate our entry (or our preference) is for *diamonds* rather than hearts. The theme of signalling preference for particular suits in this way is very common.

Love All. Dealer East.

♠ 4
♥ KJ43
♦ AQ1094
♣ KJ3

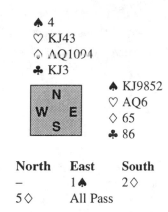

♠ KJ9852
♥ AQ6
♦ 65
♣ 86

West	North	East	South
–	–	1♠	2♦
3♠	5♦	All Pass	

West leads ♠A against South's 5♦ contract and East wants to show his partner that a heart switch is required. The best way to do this is to play an *unnecessarily* high card (♠J or even ♠K). Alternatively, if East wants a club switch, follow with ♠2. It is logical that middling cards, like ♠9 or ♠8 show no strong desire for any other suit and, therefore, by inference, encourage a spade continuation.

This is another way to tell partner what to do:

North/South Game. Dealer West.

♠ KJ93
♥ 1074
♦ AQ10
♣ AQ10

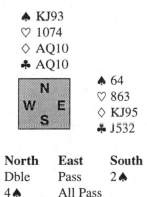

♠ 64
♥ 863
♦ KJ95
♣ J532

West	North	East	South
1♥	Dble	Pass	2♠
Pass	4♠	All Pass	

West leads ♥K, requesting count and you follow dutifully with the ♥3, showing an odd number. At trick two, partner continues with ♥A and you...?

Your *normal* card would be ♡6, so you have an opportunity to signal if you play something different. Follow with ♡8 (partner will know you have another card because of your play at trick 1) to signify a strong desire to have a switch to diamonds, the higher ranking alternative. You are using an 'idle' card.

East/West Game. Dealer South.

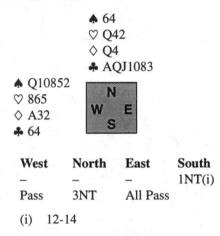

                ♠ 64
                ♡ Q42
                ◇ Q4
                ♣ AQJ1083

♠ Q10852
♡ 865
◇ A32
♣ 64

West	North	East	South
–	–	–	1NT(i)
Pass	3NT	All Pass	

(i)   12-14

You lead ♠5 (your fourth highest) and are pleased to see East produce ♠K, which declarer allows to hold. At trick 2, East continues with ♠J, again ducked by declarer whilst you follow with ♠2 to confirm a five card suit. At trick 3, East plays ♠9, won by declarer's ace and you …? To show that your entry is in *diamonds* you play ♠8 (your lowest spade outstanding).

It is clear in this example that clubs are not in the reckoning but, if they were, we could become even more sophisticated, i.e.

  ♠Q asks for hearts
  ♠10 asks for diamonds
  ♠8 asks for clubs

In our next example we can be more effective than Grecian 2000 in saving our partner a few grey hairs:

North/South Game. Dealer South.

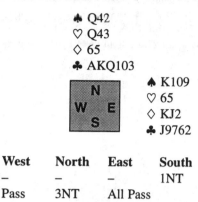

♠ Q42
♡ Q43
◇ 65
♣ AKQ103

♠ K109
♡ 65
◇ KJ2
♣ J9762

West	North	East	South
–	–	–	1NT
Pass	3NT	All Pass	

West leads ◇4 to your king which holds the trick. You return ◇J which also wins, partner following with the ◇3. A third round is taken by declarer with the ace, who immediately sets about clubs.

Partner follows to the first club, but then has to find some discards. This is *your* opportunity to help him by playing your idle clubs in a way to indicate you hold spades. After playing ♣2 initially, (you must *always* confirm the situation in the suit first, by showing your length), play ♣9 on the second round to tell West you have the higher ranking suit. If he is facing a difficult decision, that will assist him.

Be vigilant in situations where partner's 'natural' defence will meet with disaster.

Love All. Dealer West.

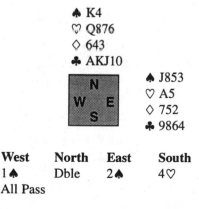

♠ K4
♡ Q876
◇ 643
♣ AKJ10

♠ J853
♡ A5
◇ 752
♣ 9864

West	North	East	South
1♠	Dble	2♠	4♡
All Pass			

West leads ♠A and you have to decide how to defend. If you play ♠3, discouraging a spade continuation, partner will almost certainly switch to a *diamond* (the logical play looking at dummy). To avoid that, you must play ♠8 to draw partner away from what might be a fatal play. It is not that you are encouraging spades, more that you are discouraging the obvious alternative. Hopefully, West can work it out from there.

Our final example demonstrates how we can use the opposing trump suit to help us:

Game All. Dealer South.

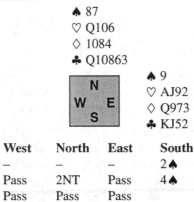

♠ 87
♡ Q106
◇ 1084
♣ Q10863

♠ 9
♡ AJ92
◇ Q973
♣ KJ52

West	North	East	South
–	–	–	2♠
Pass	2NT	Pass	4♠
Pass	Pass	Pass	

West leads ♣7 to your jack and declarer's ace. Four rounds of trumps follow and then ♣9 is led (partner following with ♣4) to your king. Do you switch to diamonds or hearts?

A diamond looks the normal defence and is best on this layout:

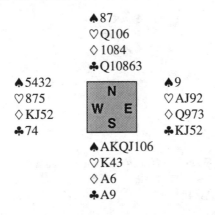

♠87
♡Q106
◇1084
♣Q10863

♠5432
♡875
◇KJ52
♣74

♠9
♡AJ92
◇Q973
♣KJ52

♠AKQJ106
♡K43
◇A6
♣A9

A low heart, which is superficially unattractive, would work in this instance:

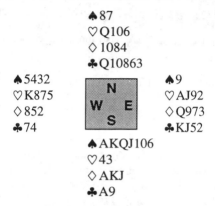

```
                    ♠87
                    ♡Q106
                    ◇1084
                    ♣Q10863
        ♠5432                      ♠9
        ♡K875        N             ♡AJ92
        ◇852      W     E          ◇Q973
        ♣74          S             ♣KJ52
                    ♠AKQJ106
                    ♡43
                    ◇AKJ
                    ♣A9
```

Which is it to be, a heart or a diamond? Is there any way to avoid a straight guess? The answer is that West should tell you by playing his spades in a particular way. In the first lay-out he can play ♠2, ♠3, ♠4, ♠5 indicating values in the lower ranking suit, whereas in the second, he should play ♠5, ♠4, ♠3 and then ♠2 showing heart preference.

Defence can only become the 'partnership' it must be, if both of you co-operate. It is hugely enjoyable, although quite demanding in the early stages, to use advanced signalling techniques.

Before we move on, let me show you how to apply these principles to your discards.

Love All. Dealer South.

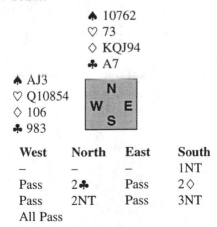

```
                    ♠ 10762
                    ♡ 73
                    ◇ KQJ94
                    ♣ A7
        ♠ AJ3
        ♡ Q10854     N
        ◇ 106      W     E
        ♣ 983        S
```

West	North	East	South
–	–	–	1NT
Pass	2♣	Pass	2◇
Pass	2NT	Pass	3NT
All Pass			

You lead ♡5, with high hopes, but partner comes up with a disappointing ♡9 and declarer wins the trick with ♡J. Next a diamond to dummy holds the trick as does ◊K at trick 3. Finally, partner wins ◊A at trick four and we have to discard. Our only hope of defeating the contract lies in spades and we must alert partner to this. How do you propose to do this?

I recommend you discard ♡Q! This simultaneously sends *three* messages:

1. It tells East that our suit is headed by the queen and 'solid' below that card.
2. It shows that declarer still has ♡AK
3. It says we do not want hearts continued, remember always discard 'rubbish', and suggests preference for the higher ranking suit (♡4 would suggest a club switch).

Not bad for one card, is it? You are hoping for a lay-out such as:

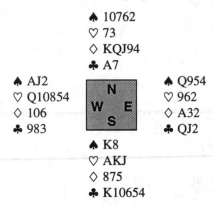

```
          ♠ 10762
          ♡ 73
          ◊ KQJ94
          ♣ A7
♠ AJ2                      ♠ Q954
♡ Q10854      N            ♡ 962
◊ 106      W     E         ◊ A32
♣ 983         S            ♣ QJ2
          ♠ K8
          ♡ AKJ
          ◊ 875
          ♣ K10654
```

A low spade switch from East should ensure four tricks in the suit and defeat the contract.

Now it is your turn to try your skill at three signalling/discarding problems:

Problem 1.

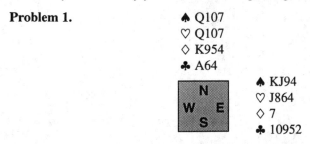

```
          ♠ Q107
          ♡ Q107
          ◊ K954
          ♣ A64
              N            ♠ KJ94
          W     E          ♡ J864
              S            ◊ 7
                           ♣ 10952
```

West	North	East	South
–	–	–	1NT
Pass	2NT	Pass	3NT
All Pass			

West leads ♣3 to your nine and declarer's jack. Next comes a diamond to the king and another diamond. Your discard ...?

Problem 2. *Love All. Dealer South.*

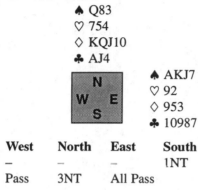

♠ Q83
♡ 754
◊ KQJ10
♣ AJ4

♠ AKJ7
♡ 92
◊ 953
♣ 10987

West	North	East	South
–	–	–	1NT
Pass	3NT	All Pass	

West leads ♡J which you discourage by playing ♡2. Declarer wins with the queen and leads a diamond to the king and follows with ◊Q from dummy. Which diamonds do you play?

Problem 3. *Game All. Dealer South.*

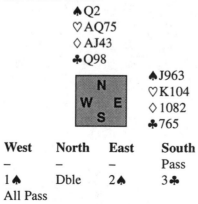

♠Q2
♡AQ75
◊AJ43
♣Q98

♠J963
♡K104
◊1082
♣765

West	North	East	South
–	–	–	Pass
1♠	Dble	2♠	3♣
All Pass			

West leads ♠K requesting the count and you dutifully follow with ♠9 (always play 2nd highest from four cards). At trick two, he continues with ♠A and you play ...?

Answers

Problem 1

♣10 (or possibly ♡4). Simultaneously we show partner our club holding and, more importantly, direct his attention to the higher ranking suit (spades). A heart discard may achieve the same, but risks giving a trick away on a layout such as this:

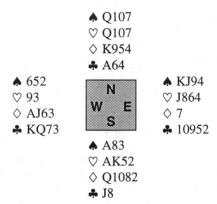

```
                          ♠ Q107
                          ♡ Q107
                          ◊ K954
                          ♣ A64
         ♠ 652                          ♠ KJ94
         ♡ 93           N               ♡ J864
         ◊ AJ63      W     E            ◊ 7
         ♣ KQ73         S               ♣ 10952
                          ♠ A83
                          ♡ AK52
                          ◊ Q1082
                          ♣ J8
```

Problem 2

◊3 followed by ◊9.

First we give partner the count in diamonds and then we play an unnecessarily high card (◊5 being the normal one to play). This should highlight our desire to see a spade land on the table. From this point it's up to partner – hopefully he has read this section.

Problem 3

♠J (or possibly ♠6 for alert partners).

Partner has cashed a second top spade, partly to ensure it does not 'run away' and partly to gain some information about our hand. We must not miss the opportunity to signal our interest in hearts by playing a high spade to catch his eye.

10
FALSECARDS
AND DECEPTION

It is one of the delights of defence when you manage to completely bamboozle declarer, by laying a series of false clues as to your distribution and/or high cards. I suppose it is the criminal mastermind in us all, which loves to plan the 'perfect crime' and get away with it. Not only that, but we get a chance to tell everyone how clever we are, without risking Her Majesty's displeasure by revealing all.

As with many 'crimes' though, we need an accomplice and at bridge he sits across the table from us. It is crucial to the success of our plan that he co-operates with us, or at least avoids 'spilling the beans'. Hence our deceptive plays in defence must be made at times when they will not be scuppered by partner. To ensure this is the case, it is wise to restrict our 'clever' plays to occasions when one of the following applies

(a) We have all the defensive strength ourselves.
(b) Partner *knows* we have made a deceptive play.
(c) Partner has no decision to make.

Then and *only then* can we have licence to kill the contract.

Here are a few examples of the more common deceptive plays:

1. Creating an Option for Declarer
Below are three suits, see if you can work out how the *East* player should play his cards (assuming the correct technique is used by declarer, South)

(a)   ♠ 73

   ♠ KQ   ♠ 1052

        ♠ AJ9864

(b)

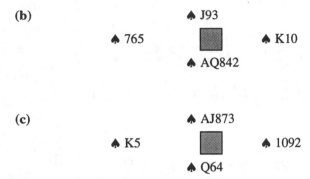

(c)

♠ AJ873

♠ K5 ♠ 1092

♠ Q64

On (a), declarer leads a low card from North and finesses ♠8 to West's queen (or king). When he next enters dummy and leads a low card, East must play ♠10 (a card he is known to hold). This will create the impression that he has ♠K102 and declarer will almost certainly finesse ♠J.

If East follows with ♠5, to the second round, he can only have one of two holdings:

    (i)   ♠K1052 *or*
    (ii)   ♠1052

In percentage terms, (ii) is more likely than (i) and an alert declarer may drop ♠K by rising with the ace. West would not be pleased ... with you!

(b) When ♠3 is led from dummy, follow with ♠K! Declarer is liable to assume this is a singleton and lead low to dummy's nine on the next round. Playing ♠10 at the first turn will result in declarer picking up the suit without difficulty.

(c) When declarer leads a low spade to dummy's jack, you must follow with ♠9 or ♠10, and not ♠2. You are trying to create this illusion:

♠AJ873

♠K52 ♠109

♠Q64

South, believing that you hold exactly ♠109 will most likely return to hand, and lead ♠Q planning to 'smother' your ten. He will be disappointed. Again, as a defender, you have nothing to lose, because you can see that normal play will result in declarer playing the suit without loss.

In all three examples, East has created a losing option for declarer where, with 'normal' play, he cannot go wrong..

2. Playing a Known Card
Let me explain the theory of *playing a known card* via the following declarer play problem:

Love All. Dealer South.

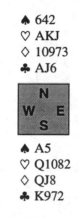

```
♠ 642
♡ AKJ
◊ 10973
♣ AJ6
```

```
♠ A5
♡ Q1082
◊ QJ8
♣ K972
```

West	North	East	South
–	–	–	1NT
Pass	3NT	All Pass	

West leads ♠K against your 3NT contract, East following with ♠3. You duck the opening lead and win the spade continuation. With four heart tricks and one spade 'in the bag', you require four clubs to make the contract.

At trick three, you finesse ♣J and are pleased to see it win. Next you cash ♣A on which West plays ♣10. Confidently you play a club to the king, dropping West's queen, and moments later score up your somewhat fortuitous game. There was little to the hand as it went, but West missed a golden opportunity to give you a difficult guess. Can you figure out what he should have done?

The key play arrived on the second round of clubs. Let us go back and consider what would happen if West followed with ♣Q, instead of the ten. Declarer concludes that West has no other clubs and finesses ♣9 on the third round, but West produces the ten and promptly cashes three spades and ◊ A K, to defeat the contract by three tricks. The full deal:

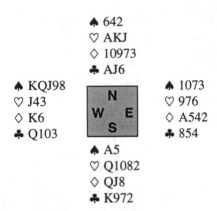

                    ♠ 642
                    ♡ AKJ
                    ◇ 10973
                    ♣ AJ6
    ♠ KQJ98   ♠ 1073
    ♡ J43   ♡ 976
    ◇ K6   ◇ A542
    ♣ Q103   ♣ 854
                    ♠ A5
                    ♡ Q1082
                    ◇ QJ8
                    ♣ K972

After the first round club finesse, West was known to hold the queen of clubs so it was a no cost play to drop it under the ace on the second round.

3. Falsecards in Trumps

It is important that we do not make our partner's life harder by our falsecarding, and hence opportunities to create deceptions are somewhat limited. However, one suit in which we are often free to express ourselves is trumps, where partner rarely has enough cards in the suit to be involved.

Here are some trump suits. You are in the East chair, and declarer leads a low card from dummy; which card should you play?

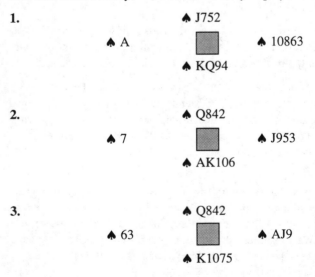

1.   ♠ J752

        ♠ A   ♠ 10863

                              ♠ KQ94

2.   ♠ Q842

        ♠ 7   ♠ J953

                              ♠ AK106

3.   ♠ Q842

        ♠ 63   ♠ AJ9

                              ♠ K1075

Answers

1. Play ♠8. When declarer's king loses to the ace, he is liable to think that West has ♠A1063:

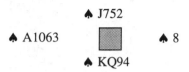

♠ J752

♠ A1063   ♠ 8

♠ KQ94

If you withhold ♠8, declarer will have no alternative but to lead to the ♠J on the next round, as he can *only* cover East having four spades.

2. Play ♠9. Exactly for the reasons above, giving the illusion that the suit is divided:

♠ Q842

♠ J753   ♠ 9

♠ AK106

Your 'falsecard' has created a situation where declarer can play *either* West or East for four trumps. Should you fail to insert ♠9, and follow 'in sleep' with ♠3, South cannot go wrong.

3. Play ♠J. Maybe declarer will next lead low to the eight, catering for:

♠Q842

♠A963   ♠J

♠K1075

Unless you try such plays, you can never succeed in being a bridge 'Houdini', and escape from seemingly impossible situations.

4. False Signals
Here is a typical defensive situation where a 'false signal' can benefit us:

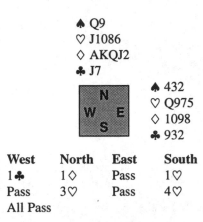

♠ Q9
♡ J1086
◇ AKQJ2
♣ J7

♠ 432
♡ Q975
◇ 1098
♣ 932

West	North	East	South
1♣	1◇	Pass	1♡
Pass	3♡	Pass	4♡
All Pass			

West leads ♣K against 4♡. We would normally follow with ♣2, showing an odd number of cards in the suit, but here we can see a chance to do something clever. If we play ♣9 and then ♣3, telling partner we have an even number of clubs, he is likely to continue the suit. Declarer believing that we are out of clubs, will probably ruff with ♡10 in dummy. He does not suspect that hearts break badly. The effect of our little deception will be to create a second trump trick for us, and thus defeat the contract.

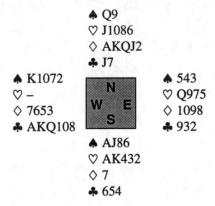

♠ Q9
♡ J1086
◇ AKQJ2
♣ J7

♠ K1072
♡ –
◇ 7653
♣ AKQ108

♠ 543
♡ Q975
◇ 1098
♣ 932

♠ AJ86
♡ AK432
◇ 7
♣ 654

Without our ruse, declarer will ruff the third club with ♡6 and then run ♡J, leaving us with only one trump trick. Once we have persuaded him to 'waste' ♡10, we can cover any heart from dummy and ensure two tricks.

A word of caution here. False signalling must be used sparingly and *only* when you have a very clear idea of your objective. It can be harmful to your partner's confidence to make such plays on a regular basis.

5.   Deceptive Leads

Back to the hot seat for our last category, the 'deceptive lead':

♠ KQJ
♡ Q6
◇ J1032
♣ KJ85

♠ 842
♡ KJ5
◇ AQ94
♣ A93

You are South, and your 1NT opener is raised to 3NT. West leads ♡2 (fourth highest) and you rise with dummy's ♡Q, which holds the trick. Next comes ◇J which you run, sadly, to West's king. He continues with another low heart which you win in hand.

Time to take stock. You have seven tricks on top and need two more. These can come by tackling spades or, if it is your lucky day, clubs. What about losers? By playing spades you will give the opponents the opportunity to cash their heart tricks. They can take ♠A, ◇K and presumably two hearts, because you expect the suit to divide 4-4 after West led ♡2 (his 'fourth best'). You lead ♠2....

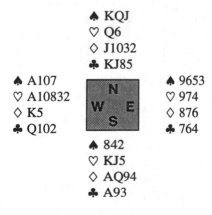

                    ♠ KQJ
                    ♡ Q6
                    ◇ J1032
                    ♣ KJ85
♠ A107   ♠ 9653
♡ A10832   ♡ 974
◇ K5   ◇ 876
♣ Q102   ♣ 764
                    ♠ 842
                    ♡ KJ5
                    ◇ AQ94
                    ♣ A93

All your careful calculations collapse around you. A happy West grabs ♠A and cashes *three* (!) hearts to defeat the contract. What is worse, clubs divided perfectly all along. You have been well and truly conned. West had realised from the bidding that his partner held next to nothing, so he was 'on his own'. In such circumstances, a deceptive lead can cause declarer to go wrong as we have just seen.

Again, as with false signals, there is a distinct *'caveat emptor'* here. You are fooling partner as well as declarer, and sometimes such tactics can backfire, particularly if partner gains the lead unexpectedly. Do not blame him if he finds the wrong line of defence. Your deception was designed to make declarer misplay the hand, you can hardly be surprised if it has the same effect on partner. However, used with discretion, deceptive plays and falsecards are valuable tools in the fight to beat contracts. Successful coups can also lead to hours of after-dinner chat, re-living your greatest moments! Seriously though, you can derive much satisfaction from carrying out your own 'Crime of the Century'.

Conclusion

We have reached the end of my 'Bridge at Home' series, and I sincerely hope that everyone has found something of benefit within it.

If you started out with *Play Bridge at Home* and have mastered everything thrown at you since then, you have much to be proud of. For those of you who already played a regular game, I hope I have added a few 'wrinkles' (to your opponents' faces, of course!). Most of all, I hope you have enjoyed the book(s) and are now panting with anticipation for your next game.

In no way have I attempted to cover all aspects of our many-splendoured pastime; that would take a series of *Encyclopaedia Britannica* proportions. However, I do feel that anyone who has taken on board the content of, in particular, this book will be a fearsome opponent in the Wednesday afternoon bridge circle.

If you wish to go further, then it is off to the local bridge club with you, and the opening of all sorts of doors. But that is another story ....